So WIDE a Sea

Essays on Biblical and Systematic Theology

edited by
Ben C. Ollenburger

Text–Reader Series 4
1991

Institute of Mennonite Studies
Elkhart, Indiana

Text-Reader Series

Series Titles:

1. *Essays on Biblical Interpretation: Anabaptist-Mennonite Perspectives* Edited by Willard M. Swartley, 1984.

2. *One Lord, One Church, One Hope, and One God: Mennonite Confessions of Faith in North America.* Howard John Loewen, 1985.

3. *Monotheism, Power and Justice: Collected Old Testament Essays.* Millard C. Lind, 1990.

4. *So Wide a Sea: Essays on Biblical and Systematic Theology.* Edited by Ben C. Ollenburger, 1991.

The Text-Reader series is published by the Institute of Mennonite Studies with the encouragement of the Council of Mennonite Seminaries. The series seeks to make available significant resource materials for seminary classroom use. By using photographic reproduction and/or desktop publishing technology, and marketing primarily through individual channels, the series seeks to make available helpful materials at relatively low cost.

Priority in accepting manuscripts will be given to material that has promise for ongoing use in the seminary classroom, with orientation toward or interest in the Anabaptist-Mennonite theological Tradition.

The Institute of Mennonite Studies is the research agency of the Associated Mennonite Biblical Seminaries, 3003 Benham Avenue, Elkhart, Indiana, 46517-1999.

Contents

Abbreviations

ANF	*Ante-Nicene Fathers*
ASBH	American Studies in Biblical Hermeneutics
CBQ	*Catholic Biblical Quarterly*
CGR	*Conrad Grebel Review*
ET	*Expository Times*
FRLANT	Forschungen zur Literatur des Alten und Neuen Testaments
HBT	*Horizons in Biblical Theology*
IDB	*Intrpreter's Dictionary of the Bible*
JBT	*Jahrbuch für Biblische Theologie*
JR	*Journal of Religion*
JSOTSS	*Journal for the Study of the Old Testament* Supplement Series
JTS	*Journal of Theological Studies*
KD	*Kerygma und Dogma*
MT	*Modern Theology*
NTA	*New Testament Abstracts*
NZST	*Neue Zeitschrift für Systematische Theologie*
OP	*Occasional Papers*
RSR	*Religious Studies Review*
SBT	Studies in Biblical Theology
SJT	*Scottish Journal of Theology*
TJ	*Trinity Journal*
TRu	*Theologische Rundschau*
TT	*Theology Today*

Contributors

Thomas Finger, Professor of Theology, Eastern Mennonite Seminary, Harrisonburg, Virginia.

Elmer A. Martens, Professor of Old Testament, Mennonite Brethren Biblical Seminary, Fresno, California.

A. James Reimer, Associate Professor of Religious Studies and Theology, Conrad Grebel College, Waterloo, Ontario.

Gordon D. Kaufman, Edward Mallinckrodt, Jr. Professor of Divinity, Harvard Divinity School, Cambridge, Massachusetts.

Mary H. Schertz, Assistant Professor of New Testament, Associated Mennonite Biblical Seminaries, Elkhart, Indiana.

Howard John Loewen, Associate Professor of Theology, Mennonite Brethren Biblical Seminary, Fresno, California.

Ben C. Ollenburger, Associate Professor of Old Testament, Associated Mennonite Biblical Seminaries, Elkhart, Indiana.

Preface

Since Scripture, by which we are led to a knowledge of God, is
very broad . . . , there is little to be gained by launching beginners
on so wide a sea.

—Gabriel Biel, 1420-95

Since Scripture is "so wide a sea," Gabriel Biel proposed to spare his students by having them study, instead, Peter Lombard's *Sentences*. According to G. R. Evans, from whom the above quotation is taken, Biel believed that Peter Lombard, in the twelfth century, had arranged the relevant, chiefly patristic material in such an orderly way that students would find in his *Sentences* the resources to settle any questions that might arise. This would remove the need of their having to consult the Bible itself.[1]

Many things have changed since the fifteenth century. Scripture remains a very wide sea, but few are now likely to share Biel's confidence that a handbook of theology would serve to measure its expanse. Already by Biel's time, and aided by his precedent, theology had begun to divide its attention between study of the Bible and 'speculative theology' (we would call it systematic theology). This division could be overcome, at least in principle, when it was the same theologian—someone like Biel or St. Thomas Aquinas—who commented on Scripture and, in another set of lectures, engaged in speculative theology. But over the past five centuries, the division of theological attention has developed into a division of disciplines, commonly allotted to different university or seminary departments. It would now be uncommon, especially in North America, for anyone to lecture on both the Bible and theology—or even on both the Old and the New Testament. Scripture itself is a wide sea, and so is the gulf dividing biblical studies and theology.

Specialization is the result of divisions like the one Gabriel Biel made, but in our day it is also one of their causes. In their pragmatic distinction between exegesis and speculative theology, Biel and his peers opened the way for scholars, several centuries later, to specialize in one or the other. It would be pointless, and I believe it would be mistaken, to argue that this specialization has produced only negative results. Specialization, by itself, is only a convenient division of labor in a common task. However, the division of labor is sometimes so rigid that it is difficult to identify the common task.

Biel could assume a world—we may think of it as a world of discourse—that encompassed Scripture, the patristic writers, a commentator like Peter

Lombard, as well as the contemporary church.   Already the Reformation
complicated this world, not only by giving Scripture a unique status, but by
making it a relatively independent object of study.   Now theology could no
longer rely on Peter Lombard, or even on patristic sources; whatever use
theology made of other material, it had ultimately to rely on Scripture itself.
By the seventeenth century, Protestant dogmatic theology had already come to
see that reliance as problematic; biblical theology emerged as an activity
oriented to demonstrating or reasserting it.   In other words, biblical theology
was simply dogmatic theology's effort to guarantee its authentic reliance on
Scripture.   But by the nineteenth century, following the Enlightenment and its
long aftermath, biblical theology confronted a choice: it could retain its orientation toward dogmatic (or systematic) theology, or it could identify itself with
the historical-critical study of the Bible.

This latter choice, which predominated, invigorated theology, but it also
raised problems that neither Gabriel Biel nor the reformers had to face.
While biblical theology retained its interest in theology's reliance on Scripture, critical study of the Bible raised serious questions about what kind of
reliance that should be, or could be.   Systematic theology raised the same
questions from within its own domain.   By the end of the nineteenth century,
systematic theology seemed to face a peculiar tension.   While historical-
critical study had to proceed in methodological independence of the Christian
tradition, in order to achieve its own historical and scientific understanding of
the Bible, dogmatic or systematic theology had somehow to depend on that
same tradition.   The strategies theologians deployed to resolve or accommodate this tension ranged across the spectrum of possibilities.   One theologian,
C. A. Bernoulli, accommodated it with a sharp consistency by proposing
parallel tracks; he identified the first as purely scientific historical research,
and the second as a practical and unscientific dogmatics that served the needs
of the church.[2]   Of course, parallel tracks do not converge.

Systematic theologians found Bernoulli's solution completely unsatisfactory.   So did Bernoulli, on subsequent reflection.   Even so, Bernoulli forced
systematic theology to find a basis on which it could be both 'scientific' and at
the same time adequate to the church's needs.   Whatever such a basis might
be—the proposals of Ernst Troeltsch and Karl Barth stand at either end of a
continuum—it would have to be found outside the historical-critical study of
the Bible (and of the church's tradition) itself.   Since this seemed to violate the
principled objectivity of historical-critical research, biblical theology's
progress to the beginning of the twentieth century implicitly (sometimes
explicitly) endorsed Bernoulli's proposal.   By then it had become wholly unclear exactly what was theological about biblical theology.   Theologians could
think of biblical scholars—even biblical theologians—as engaged in
exegetical or philological minutiae that had no positive theological importance.   For their part, biblical scholars could think of theologians as expanding
on the precedent of Peter Lombard, the title of whose work, *Sentences*

(*sententiae*), means "opinions." On the one hand, historical-critical trivia without end; on the other, mere opinions. There is no common task worth pursuing that combines trivia with mere opinion.

The past several decades have seen many efforts to correct those caricatures, and to overcome whatever truth is in them. At stake in these efforts is clarity on the question of theology's relation to the Bible. One way—it is certainly not the only way—of framing the question is to ask about the relation of biblical and systematic theology. This is the course taken by the essays in this volume. However, it proves to be a complicated course because of serious disagreements within biblical and systematic theology about the definition and task—and even the legitimacy—of each; to speak of their relation requires taking a stand on those disagreements. For that reason, the essays are also proposals in biblical and systematic theology themselves. While this is a complication, it also contributes to a genuine conversation across the boundaries—or across the "sea." It does so by requiring biblical theologians to think, not just about, but in terms of systematic theology, and by imposing the reverse requirement on systematic theologians. The success of the essays depends, in no small part, on how well they meet those requirements.

For the authors of these essays the conversation is explicitly motivated by the need to resolve issues concerning theology's relation to the Bible. This need is itself rooted in convictions about theology's relation and responsibility to the church. However, the precise nature of these convictions, and the way the issues are understood, vary among the essays. Elmer Martens, after making a case for biblical theology's "normativity" for the church, proposes a conception of systematic theology commensurate with it. He draws that conception in large part from the work of Thomas Finger, who makes his own proposal concrete by showing how classical models of atonement illumine biblical texts. A. James Reimer draws on Bernard Lonergan to argue that biblical and systematic theology are not different disciplines but different functional specialties within the discipline of Christian theology. Like Reimer, Howard Loewen draws biblical theology into the wider orbit of theology, but he does so by proposing a confessional paradigm for Christian theology. Ben Ollenburger locates biblical theology within the "logical space of normative discourse" (Jeffrey Stout), a space shared with systematic theology as an instance of the church's self-critical discursive practice. Despite significant differences among these proposals, they share convictions about the importance of theology's relation to the Bible and to the church. On the other hand, Gordon Kaufman assigns to theology a degree of autonomy that would allow it to exercise a critical responsibility in regard to both the Bible and the church; he proposes as theology's critical principle the triune God. Mary Schertz argues that biblical theology must include, and be subject to, critical analysis. She bases her proposal on feminist convictions that inform a social and ethical analysis of the power relations involved in biblical interpretation itself.

The authors of these essays are Mennonites. However, the issues they take up, and the proposals they make, are ecumenical in scope. The confessional identity of its authors reflects the origin of this book in initiatives by the Institute of Mennonite Studies to bring together biblical scholars and theologians at annual meetings of the American Academy of Religion and the Society of Biblical Literature. The essays by Thomas Finger, Elmer Martens, A. James Reimer, and Gordon Kaufman were originally prepared for those meetings, and have been revised for publication here. Kaufman's essay is a response to Reimer's. It is included, not because the editor or anyone else thought that Reimer's essay was especially in need of criticism, but because Kaufman also mounts his own argument regarding theology's relation to Scripture, and how that relation should be decided. In that respect, Kaufman's response would apply to the other essays as well.

The editor would like to thank Willard M. Swartley for his help in this project's initial stages, and the contributors for their patience and cooperation. Thanks are also due to JW Graphics and Janice Wiebe Ollenburger for help in the design and production of the book.

On this date a century ago, Karl August Wichert left the village of Fürstenwerder, near Danzig, and sailed across a very wide sea indeed. He was truly a great grandfather.

Ben C. Ollenburger
June 7, 1991

Notes

1   Evans, *The Language and Logic of the Bible: The Road to Reformation* (Cambridge: Cambridge University Press, 1985), 104.

2   Ernst Troeltsch, "Half a Century of Theology: A Review," in *Ernst Troeltsch: Writings on Theology and Religions*, ed. Robert Morgan and Michael Pye (Atlanta: John Knox Press, 1977), 77.

Chapter 1

Biblical and Systematic Theology in Interaction:
A Case Study on the Atonement

Thomas Finger

I
Introduction

Ever since the decline of neo-orthodoxy and of the "biblical theology movement," systematic and biblical theology have drifted further apart. While many lament this growing estrangement, it cannot be attributed entirely to increasing specialization, nor to the new issues that have impacted the field. Whether it arises from competition for students or publishing contracts, or from deep convictions about religion or one's own branch of study, numerous practitioners in both fields tacitly regard the other as largely irrelevant or even dangerous to their own pursuits. Accordingly, talk about constructive relationships between the two fields would be premature if it by-passed questions as to whether such relationships do or should exist.

II
Conflicts Between the Disciplines

Biblical theology is often characterized as a descriptive discipline. According to most practitioners, its major task is not to make general truth claims, but to analyze the conceptuality, imagery, theology, and style of various biblical writings within their socio-historical contexts. Consequently, biblical scholars often critique systematic theologians for indulging in generalizations that ignore or distort the particularity of Scripture.

First, biblical theologians often fault systematicians for overlooking the texts' specificity. Systematicians seldom bother to do exegesis. When particular passages offer several interpretive possibilities, they seem to select the one that fits their preconceived theory. And they seem to ignore passages that challenge these theories.

Second, systematic theology seems to reduce the rich diversity of biblical images and themes to a few fundamental motifs. Instead of marvelling at the

1

multiplicity of issues and concepts found in writings of diverse origin and purpose, systematicians seem intent on organizing as much as possible around a few that they regard as central, and disregarding all else that will not fit.

Third, systematic theology often derives its leading concepts, not from the biblical writings, but from sources such as philosophy, psychology, or comparative religion. At best, these language games are somewhat alien to those of the biblical writers, and poorly suited to express what they mean. In its strongest form, this objection maintains that the biblical perspective is so unique that other conceptualities will inevitably pervert what the writers of Scripture want to say.

However, objections such as these do not run in one direction. Systematic theology is often characterized as a constructive discipline. According to most practitioners, its major task is not to analyze the imagery of ancient texts, but to state a living faith's major truth claims in a conceptuality comprehensible for one's own day. Consequently, systematicians often criticize biblical scholars for being so preoccupied with the details of time-worn documents that they can say little to the present's urgent concerns.

First, systematic theologians find biblical theologians guilty of an absorption in minutiae that never ends. Passages are analyzed in such fine detail that the arguments can hardly be followed. No sooner have texts been painstakingly reassembled through form criticism than tradition and rhetorical and canonical criticism are rearranging them all again. Amidst the shifting avalanches of detail, any message from the text for the present seems to have vanished.

Second, systematicians regard the identification of numerous biblical images and themes as but a preliminary step. Once these elements have been isolated and placed side-by-side, the most important questions remain. Are they related to each other in certain ways? Are some prominent while others are peripheral? If these questions remain unanswered, scholars and pastors seem free to emphasize any motif that strikes their fancy, and in ways inconsistent with its original overall function.

Third, biblical scholars seem to assume that once they explain what a biblical theme meant in its socio-historical context, its meaning for the present is fairly plain. But we live in a far different world. Unless these themes can be translated into modern terms they remain largely irrelevant. In its strongest form, this objection maintains that biblical motifs are time-conditioned expressions of truths that are available to humans in other ways, and that systematic theology's task is to provide more generally accessible conceptualities (philosophical, psychological, etc.) for stating them.

Can these gulfs between biblical and systematic theology be bridged? This would be possible if one could begin on one side of the gap, affirming the basic orientation and procedures of one discipline, and yet argue that, when best carried out, these lead beyond the involuted ways in which they are often practiced—and could then call for contributions from the other discipline. Being a systematic theologian, I am tempted to argue that the concerns of my own field are (to those without prejudice) obvious, but that we could use help from biblical scholars. Partly for strategic reasons, however, and partly due to my own deep convictions, I will try to begin on the other side of the gap. In particular, I will support what I have called the strongest objection against much systematic theology—that the biblical writings express a unique perspective on reality, one that will be distorted if subordinated to more general conceptual schemes.[1] This claim, of course, is not just methodological. It is distinctly theological. It entails the rejection of what many systematic theologians affirm—that biblical motifs are time-conditioned expressions of truths generally knowable in other ways.

III
Interaction Between the Disciplines

A. *From the Bible to Systematic Conceptuality*

Starting from the uniqueness, diversity, and particularity of the biblical writings, do these writings themselves call for something like systematic theology? For the follow reasons, I would say yes.

First, most biblical writers refer to others. Jeremiah refers to Micah (Jer. 26:18). Paul mentions Peter (Galatians 2), and "Peter" mentions Paul (2 Pet. 3:15-16). Matthew and Luke know about Mark. More importantly, biblical writings quote or allude to others innumerable times. Beyond this, numerous books make reference to the same events and themes: for example, exodus, exile, resurrection, parousia, God's judgment, God's love. To be sure, different texts speak of these in different—sometimes vastly different—ways; the distinctiveness of each must be allowed to stand. Nonetheless, from a purely literary standpoint distinctiveness is not best discovered by treating writings or themes as isolated instances. Their particularity, in other words, can be fully appreciated only through asking (among other things) what they have in common.

This consideration does not yet bring us to systematic theology—to a discussion that articulates broad biblical truth claims in contemporary terms. But at least it argues the need for a full-blown biblical theology—for comprehensive comparisons and contrasts of what all the canonical writings say on common themes. And it challenges the assumption that the particularity of biblical texts and images can be discovered through concentrating on that particularity alone.

Second, all biblical writings, so far as I can see, claim to speak of ultimate realities—about God, salvation, etc. And ultimate realities, however well a particular text may claim to express them, by definition transcend whatever any one text can say. In other words, in the very attempt to speak of the ultimate, one points to a reality so comprehensive that it cannot be exhaustively defined in that single attempt. By its very nature, then, any one such expression acknowledges, at least tacitly, that other expressions from other vantage points are possible. This leaves open the possibility that essentially the same things can be expressed from different perspectives in different contexts, and that it is legitimate to ask what those same things may be.

In particular, many New Testament texts claim that God's definitive eschatological act has taken place.[2] To be sure, they differ in explaining how the "already" of this act is related to its consummation, which has "not yet" occurred. Nevertheless, none of them understands the eschaton as the abolition of earthly history, as Rudolf Bultmann has claimed.[3] Instead, the eschaton has brought, is bringing, and will bring coherence and continuity among all God's purposes for human history and the cosmos. All dimensions of reality are affected by such a claim. Accordingly, it is permissible at least to ask how any dimension—sociological, scientific, etc.—is related to and shaped by that ultimacy toward which these New Testament writings point. In other words, the claims of these writings legitimate systematic theology as a *quest*—as the search, in their light, for coherence, comprehensiveness, and synthesis among everything we can know. At the same time, of course, the biblical writings' variety and particularity place limitations on the completeness and conceptual uniformity with which this can be done.

Third, studied in their socio-historical particularity, many biblical documents, including all New Testament ones, prove to have a missionary thrust. Indeed, the more the particularity of their images and themes is appreciated, the more does it prove to arise from their intention to express their message in new situations and cultural settings. However, any deliberate effort to express something in one particular culture or thought-world acknowledges at least tacitly that other expressions are possible. And it opens the possibility that the same things can be expressed in other and later contexts—as systematic theology seeks to do. In analyzing various writings as productions of different communities, biblical scholars may sometimes forget that these were usually communities-in-mission; that is, they were not freezing the gospel into one limited cultural expression, but were outworkings of a trajectory that was opening paths for further and different translations. Ultimately, this trajectory aimed toward every person in every culture, under-girded by the assumption that the basic gospel claims could be expressed in all of them.

Finally, the path from biblical to systematic theology becomes apparent when we approach Scripture as canonical criticism recommends. First and foremost, the biblical writings are documents of a living religion, not simply records of ancient cultures. As a canonical whole, they have revitalized and transformed churches in widely diverse cultural settings for centuries. In other words, understood functionally and within their overall operating context, the images, themes, and concepts of scripture exhibit an "adaptability" and a range of "resignification" that stretches well beyond their socio-historical origins.[4] They prove to harbor latent meanings that emerge fully only in different contexts. Accordingly, systematic theology's task—to inquire after those meanings that transcend Scripture's original contexts and are expressible in the terminology of others—is legitimated by the Bible as a living canon.

Starting from their uniqueness, diversity, and particularity, I have argued that the biblical writings, understood as eschatologically ultimate, as missionary and as canonical documents, legitimate not only descriptive study of them within their socio-historical contexts, but also constructive statement of their deepest meanings in the language of many other contexts. This latter task will make some use of extra-biblical languages (such as philosophy, later church tradition, or comparative religion). I have already asserted, however, that the biblical writings express a unique perspective on reality—one that will undergo distortion if subordinated to, or reinterpreted in terms of, other language games. But given this assertion, which many biblical scholars support, how can any use of extra-biblical concepts be possible?

B. From Systematic Conceptuality to the Bible

Beginning from a given culture's conceptualities—philosophical, social, psychological, or any other—what links with biblical themes might one expect to find? Discussions of this matter often tend toward two extremes. Many theologians assume that a generally accurate understanding of many issues on which Scripture speaks is available through the proper use of rational tools available to everyone. Of course, the insights of any philosophy, psychology, or other conceptuality will need to be revised and/or supplemented in light of biblical revelation. Yet all areas of human experience, and thus all concepts that accurately express them, are thought to point in roughly the same direction as the biblical writings, and in a more or less straight line.[5]

Other theologians, however, not only affirm that biblical thought-forms are unique, they add that all other conceptualities point in directions opposed to them. Extra-biblical concepts appear wholly unable to affirm what the biblical writings do, even in an incomplete or partially distorted way. Karl Barth, for instance, insists that the biblical God

> completely takes the place of everything that elsewhere is usually called 'God,' and therefore suppresses and excludes it all, and claims to be alone the truth. . . . God in the sense of the Christian Confession is and exists in a completely different way from that which is elsewhere called divine.[6]

Such an emphasis makes any use of extra-biblical concepts in systematic theology highly problematic.

I come down somewhere between these extremes. On one hand, not only does Scripture occasionally speak of "general revelation" of various kinds,[7] but many biblical writers employ concepts from other religions and philosophies to express their own views. It seems exaggerated, then, to insist that extra-biblical concepts assert something wholly other than or opposed to Scripture. It seems better to say that they can refer to the same thing, or to certain aspects of the same thing, although in partial or distorted ways.

On the other hand, I would still affirm a high degree of uniqueness for the biblical writings. For when biblical authors utilize concepts from surrounding cultures, these concepts often take on meanings quite different from their prior ones (for example, the use of *pleroma* in Col. 1:19; 2:9). When one examines parallels between biblical and other contemporary uses of images and concepts, the differences usually prove much more striking than the similarities. This suggests that the meaning of such concepts is largely shaped by the overall *contexts* in which they function. Accordingly, the more thoroughly a concept is embedded in a meaning-complex different from the biblical one, the more opposed to the biblical perspectives its actual denotations and implications will likely be.[8] However, this does not imply that most extra-biblical images and concepts, in and of themselves, point sharply away from (or toward) biblical truth. Rather, like those used in Scripture, many such concepts have various degrees of "adaptability" and "resignification." Through incorporation into different meaning-complexes, they are capable of being stretched and modified to signify a range of different things.

All this suggests how systematic theologians can utilize many philosophical, religious, and other concepts found in their cultures. Take for instance the possibility of using the legal concept of an equivalent penalty to explain the significance of Jesus' death. Theologians will be best off assuming neither that such a concept mirrors biblical truth, nor that it inevitably distorts it. Instead, they should employ such concepts as proposals, as hypotheses. They can best ask: "To what extent, and in what ways, might the concept of legal penalty be appropriate or inappropriate for illuminating the cross?" Consideration of the diverse biblical data on Jesus' death, if it is done carefully enough, will probably not lead to simple affirmation or rejection of this concept. Should a theologian eventually adopt it, its meaning will have been stretched and revised through interaction with this material.

This approach is much like those often used in the sciences. When physicists hypothesize, for example, that light behaves like waves, they are asking a question: "To what extent does light behave like waves?" This proposal is then tested by various experiments, by means of which the original wave model will almost certainly be modified and/or supplemented, or possibly even scrapped. The testing of this hypothetical model against an experimental field will seldom lead to simple confirmation or refutation of the model. Even if the model eventually be abandoned, its testing will almost always lead to a deepened understanding of the phenomena under investigation—as well as of the explanatory potential of the original model and of others that may come into play.[9]

Above, in part A. of this section, I argued that the biblical writings, despite their wide variety of concepts, contexts, and subject matter, make affirmations about common themes. I sought to show how the eschatological, missionary, and canonical thrust of these writings make necessary the translation of these affirmations into other conceptualities. Now, in part B., I have sought to show how such translation is possible, even though the scriptural perspectives tend to be in conflict with other conceptual systems. I am arguing that when extra-biblical concepts are pried loose, as it were, from such systems and used as hypotheses in flexible ways, they can bring certain dimensions of the biblical writings to light. And they can be modified through this interaction to express biblical revelation.

So far, however, my approach may seem to imply that the above patterns of interaction can simply be deduced from general methodological considerations. In reality, this general theory has emerged gradually from my wrestling with specific texts and their relationship to systematic doctrines. Moreover, it is intended, not to demarcate the roles of biblical and systematic theology with final precision,[10] but to suggest ways whereby they might profitably interact. To make my proposal clearer, and to illustrate its usefulness, let me show how it operates in reference to an issue that played a significant role in its development.

IV
A Case Study: The Atonement

In seeking to articulate the significance of Jesus' saving work, two major theories, the substitutionary and the moral influence theories, have arisen in western theology. Despite their great differences, both theories argue deductively from premises borrowed in large measure from the cultural contexts in which they arose. I will seek to show that a third approach, the so-called "Christus Victor" motif, in several ways better reflects the variety of the biblical material. I will support this claim by taking several of its major concepts and employing them in the manner I have sketched above. I hope in the process to illustrate one way whereby biblical and systematic theology might profitably interact.

A. Traditional Theories of Atonement
Until the late 1930s, most western theologians assumed that a genuine theology of atonement was first articulated in Anselm of Canterbury's *Cur Deus Homo?* Of course, they knew that a dramatic, apparently mythological portrayal of the atonement had been widespread for about a millennium before that. According to this "Christus Victor" motif, Jesus brought salvation by defeating Death and the Devil, thereby releasing humankind from their grip. However, Anselm insisted that basing one's faith on such picturesque images was like painting pictures in the air. He sought to ground his beliefs in

something more solid—in necessary reasons that would show why atonement had to occur.[11] Without doubt, Anselm himself was steeped in Scripture; yet, in introducing the two books that make up *Cur Deus Homo?* he emphasized his fundamental method in this way:

> The first . . . leaving Christ out of view (as if nothing had ever been known of him) . . . proves, by absolute reasons, the impossibility that any person should be saved without him. Again, in the second book, likewise, as if nothing were known of Christ, it is moreover shown by plain reasoning and fact that . . . all things were to take place which we hold in regard to Christ.[12]

At the end of these efforts, Anselm's discussion partner, Boso, affirms that, "in proving that God became human by necessity, leaving out what was taken from the Bible . . . you convince both Jews and Pagans by the mere force of reason."[13]

Anselm seeks to deduce the atonement's necessity from premises concerning God's nature and governance of humankind. But while he sincerely thinks that they are universal, these premises are clearly influenced by feudal notions of honor and obedience, as well as by the philosophical and ecclesiastical traditions of his time. These premises run approximately as follows.[14] Since God is the sovereign ruler, God's purposes cannot fail; but neither can God let any transgression go unpunished. God has ordained that at least some humans will attain eternal life. Eternal life is to be merited by perfect obedience; one disobedient act, however, earns eternal death. Obedient acts performed by God are worth infinite merit.

To these general premises Anselm adds the claim that everyone has disobeyed. Everyone, therefore, deserves eternal death. Yet God has ordained that some will find eternal life, and this purpose cannot fail. Therefore, since humankind must obey God to merit eternal life, some human must render God perfect obedience. Moreover, since all have disobeyed and deserve eternal death, these transgressions must be so punished. Yet humankind's collective penalty is so great that only a person of infinite value—that is, God—can pay it. In this way, Anselm finally deduces that a divine-human person must win our salvation.

Soon after Anselm developed this "substitutionary" explanation, Peter Abelard put forth a "moral influence" theory of atonement. Yet this approach never gained the upper hand until Protestant liberalism championed it in the nineteenth century. For our purposes, it is significant that this theory, too, was often deduced from contemporary notions of morality and of God's governance of the cosmos.[15] Horace Bushnell's *The Vicarious Sacrifice* abundantly demonstrates that he was steeped in Scripture. Methodologically, however, Bushnell deduced much of his theory from a universal law of vicarious love. This law affirms that any

> good being is . . . ready, just according to his goodness, to act
> vicariously in behalf of any bad, or miserable being, whose
> condition he is able to restore. . . . Love is a principle essen-
> tially vicarious in its own nature, identifying the subject with
> others, and taking upon itself the burden of their evils.[16]

Now this love has priority even over God. For God "does not make the law of love. . . . It is with him as an eternal, necessary, immutable law, existing in logical order before his will, and commanding, in the right of its own excellence, his will and life."[17] From this law, then, one can deduce that God must come into our world, and take the burden of our sin and sorrow upon himself. Bushnell also deduces from this law other features of Jesus' atonement Since love is a moral power, God will win us, not through threat of punishment, but by inducement and attraction.[18] Bushnell does make room for God's judgment, but he deduces this from God's justice, an attribute that he defines quite differently from love.[19]

Despite great differences between these theories, they exhibit one striking methodological similarity. Both claim that an interlocking scheme of rational concepts lays bare the universal truths that underlie the varied expressions of Scripture. Neither theory acknowledges that what reason perceives might need to be modified by the biblical writings. (Of course, neither system of concepts would have been discovered, or attained its specific shape, apart from Scripture. Yet, neither theory admits this or acknowledges any possible discrepancy between its clear rational principles and the biblical data.)

To be sure, both theories helpfully articulate certain kinds of biblical data. However, taken by itself, each rational scheme also omits, and thereby distorts, some important scriptural emphases.[20] For example, while Anselm ultimately roots atonement in God's salvific will,[21] divine love is largely absent from his scheme. Without this balancing emphasis, it is scarcely surprising that Anselm's overwhelming stress on eternal punishment for even the slightest misstep has often led to an understanding of atonement chiefly as vicarious punishment, and as a message about human sin.[22]

On the other hand, despite Bushnell's admirable focus on divine love, his system of concepts also distorts it. In making vicarious love a law that even God must obey, the wonder of the divine initiative is diminished. The atonement as an act of grace—as something that God did not "have to" do, especially in light of our resistance—tends to be minimized.

These brief discussions have, I hope, clarified my claim that extra-biblical concepts can illumine dimensions of the canonical writings that may otherwise remain obscure—but also that, to the extent that they are not modified by the biblical data, they lead in directions generally opposed to its central emphases. Next, in contrast to these two partial distortions, I want to illustrate how an approach that treats such concepts as modifiable hypotheses can better illumine the uniqueness, diversity, and particularity of Scripture.

B. *The Christus Victor Motif*

Ever since Gustaf Aulen's publication of *Christus Victor*, this ancient, dramatic approach to atonement has received much attention. However, few systematic theologians have utilized it as a major theme. For the most part, they refer to it in episodic and rhetorical fashion. This is probably due to factors that have always hindered its recognition as an authentic theological explanation.[23] First, there is the strange character of Jesus' opponents: Sin, Death, Principalities, the Devil. How can the rational enterprise of theology explicate the nature of these apparently fantastic entities? Second, the Christus Victor motif abounds in paradox. One the one hand, God seems to be on the side of the powers, for they execute God's judgment on sin. On the other hand, God seems to be against them, for Christ liberates us from their bondage. Third, it has often been unclear precisely how this liberation takes place.

These last two issues spawned some apparently strange explanations, even in patristic times. Some argued that the Powers' rule over humankind was legal: in their willingness to obey them, all humans have surrendered to their rule. Accordingly, Satan did not have to let his captives go unless he was paid a ransom of at least equivalent value. Foreshadowing Anselm, some proposed that Jesus, being divine, was worth at least as much as all other humans, and that the Devil accepted him as payment in their place. In this version, a substitutionary element appears, although the penalty is paid to Satan.[24] Other theologians, however, vigorously protested this explanation. They insisted that Satan is a robber and usurper, and that God could not owe him anything.

This explanation was sometimes intertwined with the seemingly stranger notion of the deception of the Devil. Some argued that the Devil would never have sought to take Christ captive had he known who he really was. So "to him who demanded a ransom for us," God "concealed himself under the veil of our nature;" Christ's humanity formed the bait, as it were, concealing his Deity, which was the hook. Like a greedy fish, Satan lunged for the bait, but he found himself struggling with God, whom he was not powerful enough to hold. In this way, Jesus and all who would be joined to him passed out of Satan's dominion.[25]

C. *Christus Victor and Systematic Theology*

If the notions of the ransom and the Devil's deception be understood as rational explanations, combining them into a consistent theory seems very strained, if not impossible. How shall we reconcile the assertions that Jesus freed us by paying his life to his captor, and also by escaping from his grasp? And how can one maintain that God used deception at the heart of the atoning work?

I suggest that profound meaning can be discovered in these notions if we treat them, not as clear-cut concepts, intelligible part from the biblical data, but as flexible hypotheses, which only make sense when employed in dialogue with scriptural material. Let us take the strangest one of all, the deception of the Devil, and ask whether it can illumine anything that the biblical writers are saying. However, let us not insist on a perfect fit between any preconceived understanding of this notion and all the scriptural data. Instead, let us be open to modifying and filling out our initial concept in light of this data, so that it might yield further insight into what the writers are saying.

If systematic theologians ask whether so strange a notion is found in Scripture, it will force them to ponder carefully how the biblical writings speak. For although this notion has apparently functioned in theology as a strained explanation of legality (to show how Satan could be paid his ransom, yet still be legitimately overcome), if it exists in Scripture it may not be found in that form at all. Since it forms the climax of a deadly struggle, it may more likely function as one element of an overall drama or narrative—and perhaps such a narrative could be expressed in several ways. Moreover, if theology is to ask what the Bible says about the demonic, it would be good not to look primarily for clear propositional statements. For whatever the demonic may be, it is probably not entirely rational; and in any case, biblical narratives and images often communicate, among other ways, on intuitive, emotional, and aesthetic levels.

1. The Hiddenness Theme. With these broad considerations in mind, systematic theologians might first ask whether anything like Jesus' "disguise" is mentioned in connection with his death. Well, there is 1 Cor. 2:8: "None of the rulers of this age understood [God's hidden wisdom], for if they had, they would not have crucified the Lord of glory." And there is also Acts 13:27: "those who live in Jerusalem and their rulers, because they did not recognize him or understand the utterances of the prophets . . . fulfilled these by condemning him."[26] According to these texts, Jesus was executed by those who misidentified him. However, these are not Death and the Devil but earthly rulers, representing supernatural powers (according to Paul) and supported by the general populace (according to Acts).

Having located these brief assertions, systematicians might next ask whether other texts or themes point in the same direction—although perhaps with different imagery. Do other biblical writings speak of Jesus being unrecognized? The answer, clearly, is yes. There is the much-discussed 'messianic secret' in Mark. To be sure, this motif is not perfectly synonymous with that of Satan's deception, for here it is the demons who *do* know who Jesus is. Yet Mark profoundly impresses upon us how thoroughly the messianic way of redemption, with its humility, servanthood, and suffering, contradicts the human striving for position, power, and success. The crowds, Jesus' opponents, and even his own disciples remain blind as to who he really is and what his mission is about.

Many have noted that this Markan theme is similar to Paul's "theology of the cross." For Paul, also, the weakness and foolishness of Jesus' cross contradict, and are hidden from, the world in its longing for power and wisdom. This motif is presented most forcefully at the beginning of 1 Corinthians—the very place where the rulers of this aeon are said to have crucified Jesus because they did not know what the true wisdom and glory that he embodied were all about. An important similarity of theme exists, then, between the overall emphasis of Mark and the text about the rulers of this world being deceived (1 Cor. 2:8), whatever differences there may be in imagery, style, vocabulary, audience, etc.

That Jesus and his mission were unrecognized is also emphasized in other gospels. Luke repeatedly stresses a blindness theme: Jesus' contemporaries and followers could not understand the significance of Scripture, and how it pointed to fulfillment in his ministry. When the crowds, Romans, and religious rulers put Jesus to death, they knew not what they did (Luke 23:24; cf. Acts 3:17). Seen against this broader background, Acts 13:27 appears, not as an isolated proof-text, but as an expression of a very broad motif. John also represents the crowds and disciples as continually missing the deeper significance of Jesus' words and deeds. Among other things, they are puzzled by his strange talk of being "lifted up." This phrase, however, affirms that Jesus' crucifixion, in its deeper, hidden meaning, was also his glorification. Much as in Mark and Paul—despite great differences of imagery, style, etc.— we hear that God's true glory is hidden in humiliation. And John also connects this lifting up with the defeat of the Prince of this world (John 13:31-32; cf. 14:30-31; 16:11).

2. *Isaiah's Servant.* Though biblical scholars may well find other and more varied expressions of Jesus' hiddenness, I content myself with one more. This emphasis is very pronounced in Isaiah's servant theme. Many biblical theologians (and, so far as I can tell, most systematicians) think that this motif influenced various New Testament understandings of atonement. However, others disagree. Morna Hooker, for instance, will grant that this theme was influential only where "the nature of the Servant's sufferings and of their atoning value" is expressed.[27] But she cannot find this substitutionary emphasis in many references to the Servant songs.

I would argue, however, that the pervasiveness of the hiddenness theme in these songs helps show that and how they influenced the New Testament. The varied expressions of hiddenness discussed above surely indicate something significant about Jesus' historical ministry. Jesus' followers must have been deeply confused as to the meaning of his path, until his resurrection began to shed some light. But as their eyes began to be opened, they could hardly have failed to be impressed by texts expressing something so similar to their recent experience. Much as Jesus' significance was hidden from his contemporaries, so was the Servant's obscured by his humble appearance and his fate (Isa. 42:2-3; 49:7; 50:6; 52:14; 53:2, 7). Much as Israel had participated, actively or passively, in Jesus' condemnation as a blasphemer, so those in the Servant's day had "esteemed him stricken, smitten by God" (Isa. 53:4; cf. vv. 3, 8). Yet unexpectedly, like the early converts, the Servant's contemporaries had been astonished at the outcome of events: he was "exalted and lifted up" (52:13), much as Jesus was raised. This wholly unforeseen reversal would startle kings and nations (49:7; 52:15). Consequently, for both the Servant's and Jesus' contemporaries, the whole chain of events engendered an overwhelming conviction of their complicity in his death, and the heartfelt confession: "Surely he has borne *our* grief and carried *our* sorrows . . ." (53:4; cf. vv. 5, 6; Acts 2:36-37).

I am arguing that the major theme that the New Testament writers took from Isaiah's Servant songs was not substitutionary suffering pure and simple. It was the hiddenness motif, which includes the unjust but largely unwitting murder of one whose mission was hidden. In other words, the Servant songs and their New Testament adaptations express something better conceptualized in Christus Victor than in substitutionary terms. This suggests that the earliest understanding of atonement may have been expressed, not by particular sub-stitutionary or sacrificial images, but in terms of a broad, conflictive drama. That Jesus bore our griefs and transgressions may first have come to light, not as the primary meaning of his work, but as one implication of his overall mission of justice (cf. Isa. 42:1-4), his murder by enemies, and his final vindication by God. All this indicates that scholars like Hooker, who find sparse evidence of Isaiah's Servant in the New Testament, have overlooked the overarching narrative in which Isaiah's substitutionary phrases are found.[28]

All of this can explain how the early chapters of Acts can be filled with references to Isaiah's Servant, and yet how substitutionary motifs are virtually absent from the book. This fits with Luke's emphasis on the significance of Jesus' ministry for issues of justice and judgment, and mission to the gentiles. Accordingly, Acts does not develop the substitutionary features of the Servant motif (except, perhaps, in 20:28). Nevertheless, this shows how the church very early emphasized the texts from which these features could quickly arise. In any case, I think that investigation conducted in light of the Christus Victor motif challenges the common assertion that the crucifixion has "no soteriological significance" anywhere in Acts.[29] Only if 'soteriology" is iden-tified with substitutionary (or even moral influence) themes can be this be so. But if the judicial murder and divine vindication of Jesus is soteriological—perhaps in the term's most fundamental sense—Acts is shot through with soteriology.

D. Conclusions.

Let me summarize the implications that the kind of research I am suggesting would have for that traditional theme, the deception of the Devil. Systematicians can best utilize "the Devil," not as a precise concept taken from some specific cultural context, to which references to Satan, the Prince of this world, etc., can alone correspond; but, rather, more flexibly, as a pointer toward evil's activity in various forms. If they do this, they will find that demonic powers, religious and political leaders, Jesus' followers, and the crowds all misunderstood the purpose of his coming, and consequently collaborated in his crucifixion. Now this gives some concrete meaning, first, to this apparently mythological personage. "The Devil" operates, at least in large part, through social and religious structures, through collective group pressures, and through the values and life-orientations that oppose God's way of servanthood.[30]

Second, the texts describing this drama of opposition throw light on the notion of deception. All who participated in Jesus' murder indeed misunderstood him and the purpose of his mission. But why? Was it because God put on a "disguise" and appeared other than God is? On the contrary. It was because God appeared as God truly is. Because God came in humility, as a servant, as loving, as forgiving—and because these were so unlike what Jesus' contemporaries thought of as God—they were deceived. Jesus' opponents were not deceived because God tricked them; they were deceived by their own assumptions about those values that really govern the universe and characterize its Governor.

In other words, Jesus' "disguise" was not his humanity, pure and simple, which covered up his deity. It was his lowliness, his humility, his "form of a servant" (Phil. 2:7), which hide God only from those who cannot recognize him in this form. Long ago, Irenaeus recognized that God conquered the Evil One, "not by violent means, as it has obtained dominion over us at the beginning, when it insatiably snatched away what was not its own, but . . . as became a God of counsel, who does not use violent means. . . ."[31] Mennonites have also insisted that God works in this way. Yet we have often restricted this emphasis to ethics. I am suggesting that the apparently offensive notion of the Devil's deception places this emphasis at the heart of the atonement itself.

V
Summary

Biblical theologians often criticize systematicians—rightly—for subordinating the uniqueness, diversity, and particularity of biblical texts to general conceptual schemes that distort their meaning. Nevertheless, the eschatological ultimacy, missionary thrust, and living canonical function of these texts demand that their message be articulated in conceptualities other than those of their original socio-historical situations. Yet the execution of this systematic task is problematic, for extra-biblical conceptual schemes tend to move in directions opposed to those of biblical revelation. This task can be accomplished, however, if extra-biblical concepts are utilized, not as pre-defined categories to which scriptural themes must be conformed, but as flexible hypotheses in light of which the messages of the canonical writings can be examined. When employed in this fashion, the questions that these hypotheses pose can illumine previously hidden meanings and relationships among the biblical data. At the same time, the answers yielded by Scripture can revise and modify the hypotheses, molding them into suitable conceptualizations of that data.

The problems involved in subordinating biblical writings to pre-defined categories can be observed in the substitutionary and moral influence interpretations of atonement. While each theory illumines certain dimensions of this biblical theme, the inner logics of their conceptual schemes lead in directions that distort it. However, due to its intrinsically dramatic and paradoxical character, the Christus Victor motif invites systematicians to utilize its conceptuality in more flexible and hypothetical fashion. Such apparently irrational notions as the ransom paid to the Devil and the Devil's deception, when employed as suggestive pointers to a variety of biblical expressions, disclose surprising commonalities among a number of apparently diverse images and narrative themes.

Hopefully, our somewhat detailed examination of the "hiddenness" theme has also shown how biblical texts can be illumined, not only by focusing on their particular concepts and contexts, as biblical scholars are wont to do, but also be examining them in light of broader concepts and issues from other cultural settings. If Jesus' work can be clarified by notions so strange as the Devil, deception, and ransom, it can surely be usefully investigated in light of many others. Ultimately, this paper is intended, not to define the roles of biblical and systematic theology with finality, but to propose a methodology for their fruitful interaction.

Notes

1   I do not, however, assert this simply as a dogmatc presupposition. I would argue that it can be established inductively from a careful examination of the Bible's major themes and from repeated comparisons of them with extra-biblical conceptual schemes. As will shortly become clear, however, this does not imply that all such schemes are wholly false, and it allows the possibility that some might be more compatible with the biblical framework than others.

2   The following outlines my argument for the role of systematic theology in Christian Theology: An Eschatological Approach, 2 vols. (Scottdale, PA: Herald Press, 1987, 1989), 1:31-46.

3   "the end is not the completion of history but its breaking-off. . . . The old world will be replaced by a new creation, and there is no continuity between the two Aeons. . . . In the new Aeon . . . times and years will be annihilated, and months and days and hours will be no more" (Bultmann, History and Eschatology [New York: Harper & Brothers, 1957], 30). For a rejection of this catastrophic apoctalypticism, see Finger, Christian Theology, 1:110-

13, 118-20; John Howard Yoder, *The Politics of Jesus* (Grand Rapids: Wm B. Eerdmans, 1972), 36, 108-9.

4   James Sanders, *Canon and Community* (Philadelphia: Fortress Press, 1984).

5   The intertwining of 'natural' and 'revealed' theology in Thomas Aquinas is a classic expression of such a relationship. In recent discussions of theological method, Gordon Kaufman recommends beginning by constructing a concept of "world" in a philosophical way. Though Kaufman goes on to construct a "God" concept that relativizes and reconstructs this "world," he insists that the criteria involved in the latter task must also be universal and public (*An Essay on Theological Method* [Chico, CA: Scholars Press, 1975]). Cf. my own discussion and critique in "Is 'Systematic Theology' Possible from a Mennonite Perspective?" in *Explorations of Systematic Theology from Mennonite Perspectives*, ed. Willard Swartley' OP 7 (Elkhart, IN: Institute of Mennonite Studies, 1984), 37-55.

6   *Dogmatics in Outline* (New York: Harper & Brothers, 1959), 36.

7   Finger, *Christian Theology*, 1:247-55.

8   Ibid., 346-47, 252-55.

9   See Finger, "Is 'Systematic Theology' Possible?" 50-53.

10   While biblical theology seeks to describe what the biblical writings meant in their original contexts, and systematic theology seeks to interpret what they mean in the present context, no sharp dividing line can be drawn between them. For in explaining what Scripture meant, biblical theologians, too, must utilize the languages of the contemporary context; the greater the number of texts, images, and writers they seek to cover, the more must they select and interpret as systematicians do. Systematic and biblical theologies, then, both lie on the continuum that stretches between original and present contexts, although they are oriented toward the opposites poles (see Finger, *Christian Theology*, 1:57-60.

11   *Cur Deus Homo*, in *St. Anselm: Basic Writings* (LaSalle, IL: Open Court, 1962), 182-83.

12   Ibid., 177-78.

13   Ibid., 287-88.

14   See Finger, *Christian Theology*, 1:304-8.

15   Ibid., 1:311-14.

16   *The Vicarious Sacrifice*, vol. 1 (New York: Charles Scribner's Sons, 1903), 41-42.

17   Ibid., 308; cf. p. 235.

18   Ibid., 154; cf. pp. 160, 403-04.

19   Ibid., 233-95.

20   Cf. Finger, *Christian Theology*, 1:346-48.

21   I disagree with Gustaf Aulen's criticism that atonement for Anselm is achieved primarily by Christ "as man," and not by God. See *Christus Victor* (New York: Macmillan, 1960), 81-100.

22   J. Denny Weaver highlights Anselm's emphasis that Jesus' crucifixion paid the penalty of eternal death, but he hardly mentions Anselm's insistence that Jesus' earthly obedience merited eternal life. While this is somewhat un-balanced as an actual account of Anselm, it does reflect the way Anselm's theory has often been understood. See Weaver's essay, "Perspectives on a Mennonite Theology," in CGR 2 (1984): 200-2. Many of my own criticisms of Anselm correspond with Weaver's (see Finger, *Christian Theology*, 1:307-08.

23   Finger, *Christian Theology*, 1:317-22.

24   Since Satan executes God's judgment, however, it can also be argued that this ransom is ultimately paid to God (see Aulen, *Christus Victor*, 56-57). For a discussion of the ransom controversy, see ibid., 47-51.

25   Gregory of Nyssa, "Address on Religious Instruction," as quoted in Aulen, *Christus Victor*, 52.

26   All quotations from Scripture are according to the RSV.

27   *Jesus and the Servant* (London: SPCK, 1959), 110.

28   For instance, when Hooker cannot find substitutionary suffering in Acts 8:32-35, where the unjust death of the servant is emphasized, she concludes that Isaiah 53 was quoted there only "as a proof-text of the necessity of Christ's passion, and not as a theological exposition of its meaning" (ibid., 114). This quotation of Isaiah 53 merely shows "how the early church was ready to make use of any Scripture which was presented to her, in order to show how Christ's work had been foreshadowed there" (ibid., 113).

29   Eduard Schweizer, *Lordship and Discipleship* (Naperville, IL: Allenson, 1960), 33; cf. Hans Conzelmann, *The Theology of St. Luke* (Philadelphia: Fortress Press, 1961), 201.

30   Although I agree with many features that J. Denny Weaver identifies in the notion of the demonic, he apparently interprets it in a "demythologized version," in which "Jesus confronts *not* personal devil *but* the conglomerate of evil present in the world. . ." (Weaver, "Perspectives," 202, emphases mine). I would insist, however, that the demonic cannot be reduced entirely to sociolog-ical terms. See Finger, *Christian Theology*, 1:331, 339-40.

31   *Against Heresies*, Book V, Chapter 1, Section 1 (ANF, 1:527).

Chapter 2

BIBLICAL THEOLOGY AND NORMATIVITY

Elmer A. Martens

I
What Is Biblical Theology All About?

Biblical theology takes as its task laying bare the theology that is in the Bible. Even in this restricted (and inadequate?) definition the question arises: to what extent are the results of such research directly relevant to the believing community? Clearly such results are of historic interest. But do the conclusions of a biblical theology have relevance in the sense of being 'normative', and if normative, normative for whom and on what grounds? Are the results of the investigations to be handed over to dogmaticians who will then rule on their normativity (the current consensus), or has biblical theology itself more immediate and direct responsibilities to the community relative to its belief and behavior, as I shall argue it does?

The purpose of this paper is to tangle with these questions, to revisit earlier answers to the question, and to nudge biblical theologians to bring the results of their work more immediately to bear on the life of the believing community, or even contemporary culture. Such an attempt may seem bold, even rash, given the never-ending squabbles about the definition of biblical theology's task, the plurality of the existing formulations, the dismal prospects of the discipline, and the fear that to take on the larger task, which leads to norming, is only to revert to the pre-Gabler era.

Several recent articles hardly offer encouragement to proceed in the direction proposed. R. N. Whybray, the British scholar, has put the legitimacy of the enterprise into question in a published essay, "Old Testament Theology: A Non-existent Beast?"[1] John J. Collins, in a paper entitled, "Is a Critical Biblical Theology Possible?" concludes, "Historical criticism, consistently understood, is not compatible with a confessional theology that is committed to specific doctrines on the basis of faith."[2] He makes room for biblical theology, not as a normative discipline, but as a sub-discipline with an analytical task whose main contribution "is to clarify the genre of the biblical material in the broad sense of the way in which it should be read and the ex-

pectations that are appropriate to it."[3] James Barr's essay, "The Theological
Case Against Biblical Theology," in the Brevard Child's *Festschrift*, throws up
a host of cautions for the discipline, and raises questions about how
"theological" biblical theology is anyway.[4]

Discussion about the question of biblical theology and normativity can
serve to focus the issue, What is biblical theology all about? That role, this
paper will suggest, rather than being secondary or tangential, should be constructive and deal more directly with what is normative or prescriptive for the
believing community. By 'normative' is meant that which is binding in charting
beliefs and behaviors. That is, biblical theology represents major input in
defining what the believing community confesses. Where, then, in a Christian
believing community a variety of factors vie in determining the shape of a
belief system, apart from the Bible itself biblical theology is a primary
arbiter. The operating presupposition is that the Bible is Scripture; the orientation here, derived from the free church tradition, is that the referent for biblical theology is the church as the first public, but that account needs also to be
taken of two other publics—the academy and general society.

II
The Debate About Normativity

The voices from the past give a mixed message on the question of whether
biblical theology has any further business beyond historical description.
Johannes Lindblom in the 1930s stated, "The scholarly study of questions of
enduring values in revelation and of similar problems of faith we gladly
leave to the theologians."[5] Similarly, biblical scholars of the nineteenth
century stressed that biblical theology had a limited function.

Reginal Fuller, in reviewing the effect of the historical method, notes,
"Instead of setting out a normative theology for contemporary preaching, New
Testament theologies became more and more descriptions of the history of
New Testament thought and religion."[6] H. H. Schultz, an Old Testament
scholar of the nineteenth century, wrote, "Biblical Theology has to show from a
purely historical standpoint, what were the doctrinal views and moral ideas
which animated the leading spirits of our religion during the Biblical period
of its growth."[7] W. A. Irwin concurred with Eichrodt: the biblical theologian
is: "concerned purely and simply with telling in organized form what Israel
believed."[8] Till today one hears that biblical theology is "a historical and
descriptive discipline rather than a normative and prescriptive one."[9]

The reluctance to say more stemmed from the "fear that biblical theology
would attempt to take on a normative role."[10] The fear arose in part from the
sense that to move into the realm of eternal values and statements of faith was
to leave behind the hard-won results in the battle about methodology. That
battle had left the historical-critical method triumphant. For the biblical theologians to venture into the field of the confessional, or for them to give

guidance on what was to be believed, was to slide into another (subjective) method. Historical-critical scholarship "held that it [biblical theology] was a historical discipline, not normative for faith. . . ."[11] John J. Collins has recently proposed a role for biblical theology that goes beyond the descriptive function but stops short of being normative. Like Wrede and others, Collins looks for an accepted commonly-held method, and while this method can assist in the necessary analytical process, it is giving too much to biblical theology to assign it a norming role.[12]

But there have been other voices that called for the discipline to do more than describe an ancient faith. In 1909, Adolph Schlatter advocated that New Testament theology be more than descriptive, that it function normatively for the church's faith and preaching. In 1921, Rudolf Kittel urged that a final objective of Old Testament scholarship be "the assertion of the enduring values of Old Testament religion and the expression of its place in the total of the divine order of the world."[13] Kittel called for some systematic presentation of the essence of Old Testament religion that could be called theological and that was of lasting value.[14] Karl Girgensohn proposed pneumatic exegesis, while retaining the historical-critical method, as a way of grasping the enduring message of Scripture. Years later, Otto Baab concluded his volume with a chapter on "The Validity of Old Testament Theology." He wrote, "The suitability of attempting to formulate an Old Testament theology which involves both description and evaluation is suggested by the need of modern men and by the fact that validity is continuously claimed by the Old Testament itself for the major beliefs which it records.."[15] In a 1981 essay on the future task of biblical theology, Claus Westermann urged theology to address itself more self-consciously to humankind and the world as a whole, and held that to do so called for an integration of the disciplines of biblical theology—historical theology, systematic theology, and practical theology.[16] More recently, Brevard S. Childs has advocated a canonical approach which, among other things, "also opens an avenue into the material in order to free the Old Testament for a more powerful theological role within the life of the Christian church."[17] There are reasons, it is here suggested, to set aside the earlier reserve, and even to make the case that biblical theology occupy itself with the question of the "normative."

A. The Dissolution of the "Meant"/"Means" Distinction

One of the reasons for biblical theologians shying away from any notion of translating their results into immediate relevance is the view that one should keep separate what the text meant from what it means. Biblical theologians should occupy themselves solely with the first, that is, what the text meant. Krister Stendahl's important dictionary essay on biblical theology was intended as a program for the discipline, as he himself later explained.[18] That program caught up the spirit of the discussion of the past decades by limiting the work of the biblical theologian to a description of what the biblical texts meant. Stendahl explained that the tools of historical criticism enabled one to explicate the text's meaning. This descriptive function of detailing what the text "meant" was to be sharply differentiated from the task of declaring what the text "means" in our situation. Such a prescriptive function, he implied, belonged elsewhere than with biblical theologians.

While such a position appears simple and straightforward, subsequent analyses have shown Stendahl's program to be encumbered with problems, so much so that Brueggemann could say in the mid 1980s: "The distinction of 'what it meant' and 'what it means,' between descriptive and normative articulations (most clearly stated by Professor Stendahl) is increasingly disregarded, overlooked or denied."[19] One reason for setting Stendahl's distinctions aside was that the historical-critical method, which was the kingpin in the descriptive task, was itself under attack. More and more it was recognized that the method was not subjectivity-free. While this observation did not invalidate the historical-critical method, it did raise the question how biases in prescribing current belief were different from biases in describing past belief. That is, the subjective element—always the problem for articulating what is normative in theology—was no longer the problem only for the prescriptive task; one could not escape it already in the earlier stage of the descriptive task. So the distinction between "what it meant" and "what it means" lost some of its force. Indeed the descriptions of meanings were, and are, not a little determined by what one believed the Bible to contain. If, as in Gabler's day, the Bible contained ideas, then the way to proceed was to describe what holy writers thought (i.e. ideas) about divine matters. Others viewed the Bible as having piety for its subject matter. A description then took the form of a 'history of religion.' Still others approached the Bible as presenting a series of events. The descriptive task could then issue in a 'history of salvation.'

There were still other determining factors at work in the descriptive task which entailed collecting and systematizing the theological data. Even within a descriptive task, how did a system or a synthesis emerge? David Kelsey argued that the synthesis arose as an act of "imaginative construal" by the interpreter.[20] The collection of material, if it was more than a catalogue, took an ordering and a shape derived not so much from the texts, if at all, but from the brain of the collector. Thus, Kelsey could use Rudolf Bultmann's work as an example of the construal of New Testament materials about the presence of God in the mode of ideal possibility. For Bultmann, the collection, arrangement, or "construal" was shaped by the scripture's statement about the Kerygma and the consequent "possibility of authentic existence."[21] In short, it was the mind of the theologian that creatively caught up the biblical material and depicted it. The configuration of the "collection" was not one demanded by the text but one created by the theologian. And in this respect, namely the imaginative construal of the data, the biblical theologian and the systematic theologian were on common ground. The distinction, then, between a description of "what it meant" and the prescription of "what it means" tended to blur.

B. Revision of the "Descriptive"/"Normative" Distinction

Further skepticism about the propriety of Stendahl's distinction centered in logic and semantics. Stendahl proposed two distinct and largely opposite modes of operation—the descriptive and the normative. But, as Ben C. Ollenburger has noted, these are not as opposite as might at first seem.[22] To begin with, the descriptive task follows certain procedures or norms. One can readily speak of a "normative description" without getting caught in contradictions. The one who describes is constrained in his or her activity by accepted understandings. Ollenburger conjectures a range of acceptable frameworks, such as the architectural or the functional, for the description, for example, of the Tower of Pisa. However, an astrologically-based description of the Tower would fall outside the recognized framework. So, norms come into play when describing, including the describing process of the Old Testament. It was an illusion that we ever thought they didn't.

What norms are there for Scripture? The historical-critical method is an accepted norm. But as Ronald Clements notes (using the messianic text of Isa. 7:14), the historical-critical method, while helpful in giving a primary "correct" meaning to a text, does not aid in giving the range of meanings.[23] The fact is that the "meaning" of this messianic text must take into account the meaning ascribed to it within the canonical literature. That is, the Matthean use of this text (Matt. 1:23) is part of what the Isaiah text means. The re-interpretation of a promise within a collection of canonical books springs the boundaries of the "correct" meaning required by the historical-critical method. In the light of this example, does J. J. Collins's statement stand, that the historical-critical method is "the most satisfactory context for biblical theology"?[24]

Ollenburger complains that in advocating the descriptive method, Stendahl allows only one angle of vision, namely the historical-critical method.[25] In any case, Stendahl has set some priorities, which is to say that he has engaged in evaluation, which in turn is to be put at the edge of normative-type questions; so one cannot speak about description without speaking about norms.

Neither can the norming process (conceding for the moment that it is a separate process) be conducted apart from description. The setting out of norms is essentially a descriptive enterprise. There is then one modality, that of description, operating for both of Stendahl's "tasks." This observation means that the distinction between the "descriptive" and the "normative" that Stendahl proposed is not at all as absolute as he thought. Ollenburger offers further critique, enough to put into question whether the "meant"/"means" distinction is valid. The distinction between what a text meant and what it means is suspect because in both stages subjectivity is unavoidable, because semantic confusion attends the distinction, and also because in doing theology, even in the descriptive mode, there is an imaginative leap.

One must admit that in the larger interpretative process we can distinguish two moments. One "moment" is the explicating of the meaning of a text given its contexts, its vocabulary, etc. Rolf Knierim rightly notes, "The descriptive task is indispensable for the theological task but it is not identical with it."[26] Another "moment" in the total interpretative process, I suggest, is the articulation of the meaning for contemporaries. The argument here is that the sharp distinctions between the two moments is not tenable, and that therefore the way is open to consider a role for biblical theology larger than the historical summary of what was once believed.

C. Changing Expectations Regarding the Tasks of Biblical Theology and Systematic Theology

1. *Arguments for a Clear Distinction.* One of the reasons for restraining biblical theologians from addressing the contemporary situation was a conviction that the two disciplines—biblical theology and systematic theology— were discrete disciplines, each with a clear-cut responsibility. It was the task of the biblical theologian to assemble in theological fashion the scholarly research and to present the results to the systematic theologian. So, for example, W. A. Irwin states that the Old Testament worker "will serve his function by bringing his results to an assimilable state and presenting them to the professional theologian in a form which can be meaningful for his studies."[27] Gerhard Ebeling is of the same opinion: "It [biblical theology] leaves entirely to dogmatics the doubtful advantage of providing normative theological statements for the present situation. . . ."[28] Dietrich Ritschl makes a similar observation: "And if such a 'synthesis' [of biblical materials] is again and again attempted and presented (as is proper), the goal of such a presentation should by no means be to deduce from these contents something normative or theologically definitive for the present."[29]

The prevailing view is that Old Testament theology or New Testament theology should hand over its findings to the doctrinal theologians. So for example, most recently Reginald Fuller notes that dialogue between dogmatics and New Testament theology is needed and proposes that the New Testament theologian, in a final chapter of his work, hand over the results of his/her work to the dogmatician.[30] Is that not saying that the raw material, like crude oil, is to be conveyed to the doctrinal theologian, who will render it into normative form, so that in this form it may power the automobile, understood as the believing community?

An immediate observation is that systematic theologians seem not necessarily to be dependent on the results forwarded to them by the biblical theologian. Krister Stendahl remarks that Paul Tillich could write a systematic theology utilizing very little biblical support.[31] In its development, process theology was initially more dependent on Alfred North Whitehead than on specific biblical materials, necessitating at a later stage a book by the title:

The Lure of God: A Biblical Background for Process Theism.[32] To be sure, other systematic theologians, of course, have been more attentive at all stages to the "results" of biblical scholars.[33] Still, it is in varying ways that systematic theologians utilize the work of biblical theologians.

It was also clear that evaluative judgments were being made by biblical theologians; what were these about if not to move toward the normative? As Hayes and Prussner note, ". . . one might argue that if a work is going to be a theological inquiry then it should have, in addition to its concern for the phenomenological or purely descriptive aspects of religion, also a definite and legitimate interest in the problem of ultimate truth and value."[34] Otto Baab held that "a consideration of the question of validity is a legitimate task for the Old Testament theologian."[35] Baab wanted the biblical theologian to do the work of a theologian: "Theology always claims, according to its adherents, to be in some sense exclusive and final in its pronouncements."[36] This view contrasts sharply with that of W. A. Irwin who cautioned, "The Old Testament worker, if he is to perform his true function, must be trained in theology and must keep himself abreast of the course of thought—always on guard, however, lest he then imagine himself a theologian!"[37]

That last remark is echoed by both J. J. Collins and James Barr. Collins observes that conclusions from biblical theology could or even ought to be compared with metaphysical systems—process philosophy, for example. But, says Collins, "It is not within the competence of biblical theologians as such to adjudicate the relative adequacy of metaphysical systems."[38] Similarly, James Barr notes that "Biblical theologians can hardly presume to instruct doctrinal theologians in what does or does not constitute theology."[39] Biblical theologians have not the necessary *material*, he says. Now most biblical theologians would concede lack of full qualification in the field of metaphysics. But is the conclusion drawn from this state of affairs valid, namely, that biblical theologians have no voice in depicting the contemporary relevance of their findings? Could it not also be argued that doctrinal theologians have not the competence needed to be biblical theologians, and that therefore they are also limited? And have they such a sure Archimedian place to stand that they can pontificate on the absolute truth? Moreover, is it not reasonable to think that the biblical theologians, occupied with the primary material of research, Scripture, are in a favored position to at least suggest how their conclusions might look, in terms of their relevance?

2. Reasons for a Common Responsibility. This position of keeping biblical theologians who want to address the question of the normative at bay, and deferring responsibility rather to doctrinal theologians, assumes a cleanly marked area of function for each. When it is here suggested that biblical theologians ought to engage in the task of setting out the norming guidelines for faith that follow from their work, it is not assumed that they, rather than the doctrinal theologians, will now have the last word about regulative faith. The burden of this paper is not to suggest that biblical theology supplant doctrinal theology. It is to say that biblical theology must take with greater seriousness the responsibility to speak to the community of faith about what is normative. It is also to say that the discrete division of labor needs to be re-examined. What if biblical theologians and systematic theologians were conversation partners?

Just how one goes about bringing greater interaction between doctrinal and biblical theologians needs further exploration. Paul Hanson describes his approach and that of Bernhard W. Anderson and Walter Brueggemann as moving "dialectically between descriptive and normative aspects of interpreta-tion. It does not seem advisable to leave the latter strictly to systematic the-ologians. . . ."40 One might well consider a restructured relationship between biblical theology and systematic theology. Rather than to visualize them as overly discrete and opposite, the two disciplines can better be plotted on a continuum. Thomas Finger has helpfully suggested that a continuum exists be-tween the kerygmatic pole and the present contextual pole. The kerygma is the gospel grounded in the Scripture. The current contextual pole is the be-lieving community for which the kerygma must be translated. "Systematic and Biblical Theologies, then, both lie on the continuum which stretches between original and present context, although they are oriented towards the opposite poles."41 In this conceptualization, both disciplines are occupied with the biblical material and both have responsibilities to the contemporary context. But there are different accents. Biblical theology will have the historical bib-lical context primarily in focus, but beyond the interpretative word it will also take responsibility for the regulative word. Doctrinal theology, focussing more on the contemporary agenda and sensitive to philosophical dimensions, never-theless draws from the biblical texts in order to delineate guidelines for the community's faith and practice.

James Barr looks askance at such interlinkage between biblical theology and doctrinal theology. It is troublesome to him that biblical theology has been in the business of trying to influence and even to direct doctrinal theology, rather than being simply ancillary. More to the point is his state-ment: "If biblical theology is to accept that it is dogmatically interlinked as a matter of principle—as in part it often is as a matter of fact—then it will have to accept that that means also a reduction of its influence and effectiveness."42 His point is that "too close an alliance with particular doctrinal trends can only damage the reputation and the effect of biblical theology."43 Barr has argued correctly that biblical theology is not really independent. And yes, biblical theology has in fact been pointing the direction doctrinal theology should go. Any linkage in principle may diminish the image of biblical theology, but more is at stake than an image. More is at stake than egotisti-cally guarding some turf. At stake are both the function of an enterprise more whollistically theological, and the responsible guidance of a community. It is the mission of theology that matters, and not the continued isolation of the dis-ciplines. Another scenario is possible, namely that by the interlinking of two disciplines there is forged a position that is to the advantage of both disciplines.

The proposal here, it should be stressed, is not to return to pre-Gabler days. Rather the proposal is for some dialogue between biblical and doctrinal theologians.[44] Models for such dialogue are scarce, but the interaction between the two disciplines in the essays printed in the annual *Jahrbuch fuer Biblische Theologie* is to be lauded.

Now the position that calls for biblical theology to be more immediately relevant, even "normative," might be challenged on the ground of "imperialism." Stendahl cautioned lest biblical theology take too much on to itself: "In restricting the primary role of the biblical scholar to the descriptive task, it was my intention to liberate the theological enterprise from what I perceived as 'the imperialism of biblical scholars' in the field of theology."[45] Stendahl conceded that biblical categories "stimulate and guide," but he considered it too forward for biblical theologians single-handedly to take to the field of the prescriptive.

In reply to Stendahl's fear of "imperialism" one should urge that modesty is becoming for any scholar or group of scholars. The results of biblical theological research are submitted for testing to colleagues and to the believing community. To advocate a role of contemporary relevance for biblical theology is not to advocate theological dictatorship by biblical theologians. For that matter, an imperialism of any sort, including that of systematic theologians, is to be resisted. With more dialogue between the biblical and systematic theologies, as envisioned here, the fear of imperialism should be largely allayed. The question is, can one not conceive of biblical theology and systematic theology in a relationship such that both work at the normative task?

III
Refined Understandings of Theology as Theory

Our subject is complicated by the ambiguity of the term "theology." Collins refers to theology "understood as an open-ended inquiry into the meaning and function of God-language."[46] James Barr admits that the discussion about biblical theology can be swung in different directions, depending in part on the definition of theology. He distinguished between theology that has the Bible for its horizon (biblical theology) and that which has God for its horizon (doctrinal theology).[47] Similarly, Ritschl identifies one definition of theology as that which is declared about God, Christ, humankind before God, etc. He himself favors a more elastic definition of theology as that which informs the actions and beliefs of a community.[48]

We have proceeded thus far with the tacit understanding of theology as that discipline which in its talk about God summarizes the essentials of the Christian faith and what ought therefore to be believed by a Christian. In such a view, theology is normative for the believing community. As Langdon Gilkey explains with reference to systematic theology, "traditional theology—mostly before the modern period—understood itself, and was understood, as stating authoritatively 'What ought to be believed,' as in that sense of setting 'norms' for belief and often for both church and society."[49] Such a definition of systematic theology needs inspection.

Whatever the reasons, and they are many, theologians do not now see their task as building a theological edifice which neatly builds together all the pieces and invites adherents of the Christian faith to take shelter in their structure. To be sure, from the tradition, it may be expected that the theologian's task is one of defining what ought to be believed. But as a matter of fact, "As a moment's reflection will clarify, this is not what goes on in a contemporary class or program in theology . . . any more than do most medical schools now center their curricula around courses in bleeding."[50] The monolithic nature of systematic theology, if it ever existed, is outmoded.

The 'normative', in the sense of theology offering eternally valid positions, is a notion not now widely advocated. In its place, as Gilkey explains, is a view of theology as theory. Somewhat comparably, Thomas Finger speaks of theological reasoning in terms of models. "A model is a well-known object, image, or process which appears to have certain points of similarity with something much less known."[51] Or again, under a section titled "The Norm and Criteria of Theology," Finger explains that theological reflection "assesses the implications and the range of different models, compares them with each other, and decides which models or combinations of models express the kerygma adequately in particular contexts."[52] Theories or models are something between the descriptive and the normative. Theology, then, is engaged in setting up propositions for testing. These propositions are tested, for example for faithfulness to Scripture, for adequacy, for clarity of articulation in a new context.

One could compare the theologian's use of theory to that of the scientist. By means of theory, the scientist seeks to take account of the data and to offer an explanation. That theory is adequate to a greater or lesser degree. In so far as the theory "works," it becomes increasingly important as a guide. That is, the theory is normative, even though admittedly it is of a provisional nature. Quite conceivably, another theory could be advanced which more adequately incorporated the data, and which would then become the new norm. The keys to validity include adequacy, consistency, and comprehensiveness.

Similarly, theology, whether it be biblical theology or systematic theology, represents a theory of how the theologumen, the components of theory, are to be understood in their relationships. Biblical theology will use the biblical data and organize its construct in biblical categories. Systematic theology, in addition to the biblical data, will handle data from church tradition and prevailing philosophical world views. The function of these theories is to articulate for a new context the meaning and the application of the kerygma. And within this function, either theology has a responsibility to offer its theories as 'normative', that is, as regulative for faith and practice.

Undoubtedly, an objection to the "normative" nature of theories is that the community of faith is confronted not with one theory but with a plethora of theories or models, both by the biblical and also by the systematic theologian. To this objection there are three responses. One response to this situation is to acknowledge that the diversity is a diversity not unlike that found in the basic document of the Scriptures. Scripture, even though its texts cannot be easily harmonized, does not cease to have binding claims on the community. Nor is the resulting variety of theories or models as norms to be dismissed simply because of the variety. A second response is that the models or theories inevitably have on them the imprint of the model-makers and the theoreticians. Ernest Best has documented well how the interpretation of a single text over the centuries has been influenced by the questions brought to it out of different contexts.[53] In a similar way we can account in part for the plurality of theories.

A further response is that there can be an ordering within multiple theories. Rolf Knierim has called for a criteria of ordering, drawn from the biblical source itself, that will adjudicate our plural theologies.[54] Recently, Paul Hanson for the Old Testament and James Dunn for the New Testament have addressed the question of diversity.[55] More recently still, John Goldingay has helpfully noted that one can deal with theological diversity by taking account of contexts, engaging in evaluations and by working constructively with the diversity.[56] Admittedly, "how such theories are testable is a tricky question and varies with the level of theory to which we refer."[57] Thomas Finger offers four criteria: coherence, logical consistency, adequacy and applicability.[58] To be sure, the plurality of theories complicates the discussion on how these theories are normative. But the complication is not sufficient reason to deny to them a regulative function.

Understanding the theologies as theories or models, while it raises problems, has some advantages: it opens the door wide for biblical theologians to be theologians. It also clarifies in what way the Bible as Scripture is the ultimate norm. Finger says, "Thus the kerygma expressed in Scripture is the sole norm of the truth of theological statements."[59] Similarly Childs asserts, "To do Biblical Theology within the context of the canon involves acknowledgement of the normative quality of the biblical tradition."[60] Theologies are articulations about the meaning of the kerygma, the Scripture. These articulations function as a derivative norm. The concept of primary norm (Bible) and derivative norms (theologies) safeguards from according finality to any statement of theology. Pride of place is given to the canon; it remains the norm in a way that theologies drawn from it do not.

IV
The Function of Canon

A nudge toward incorporating into biblical theology the task of addressing the contemporary situation arises from the fact of canon. Biblical theology has the two testaments as its primary documents. These primary documents have a particular claim on the Christian believing community. It follows, by definition, that biblical theology, which deals with the canonical material, would be entitled to lay something of a claim on those for whom the Bible is canonical. Ronald Clements notes, ". . . it is through its theological content that the Old Testament can be claimed as authoritative for us."[61] A discipline that identifies that theological content can hardly sidestep a direct responsibility to the believing community.

Such comment already implies a particular referent. When talking about meanings one cannot escape asking, "Meaning for whom?" The biblical theologian who stands within a confessional context can hardly detach his work from the believing community. "One who practices Old Testament theology, as distinct from rhetorical or literary criticism or history of religion, is likely to understand one's self as nurtured by and accountable to a concrete community of reference which has already decided some things."[62] For the biblical theologian the "community of interest," that is, the referent, is the believing community. For the systematic theologian, the "community of interest"[63] is both the church and the wider world. Not infrequently theologians, whether of the biblical or systematic variety, stand also in the context of the academy. They work as colleagues, critiquing and affirming conclusions. Brueggemann observes that the tendency in the academy is to hold commitments in "some kind of tentativeness," but goes on to say, "I think that we must recognize that doing Old Testament theology requires that such decisions of reference cannot be held in abeyance and must be acknowledged as proper to the work."[64]

The move from the mere statement of results to wrestling with the contemporary relevance for the confessional community is not unnatural. It is almost inevitable. Krister Stendahl, while urging the distinction between description and prescription, comments, "The following essays often move from the descriptive task to the development of meanings for church and society today."[65] Goldingay notes, "We are not merely reformulating the faith explicitly expressed or implicitly presupposed by a believing community of Old Testament times, in order to understand Old Testament faith for its own sake, but formulating the theological implications of that faith in a way that brings them home to us as members of a believing community in our time."[66] The scholar in the academy who may stand apart from the believing community can nevertheless render his/her students a service by pointing out the implications for a believing community.

Brueggemann, after outlining a scheme for biblical theology around the bi-polar concepts of legitimation of structure and the embrace of pain, says,

"Insofar as Old Testament theology is related to the life of the church, this way of organizing our understanding of the text may be peculiarly poignant in our cultural context."[67] Brevard Childs even suggests that contemporary concerns became agenda for the biblical theologian. After noting how both the academy and the church are "referents" for biblical theology, he remarks, "Rather, it would be far more productive if biblical theologians of various persuasions begin to work on some of the burning questions of the day."[68] He cites male/female relationships, creation, and ecology.

The direction of my argument is to lend support to the work done in the series, "Overtures to Biblical Theology." The first volume, by Professor Walter Brueggemann, for example, is not limited to the mere description of what the Old Testament has to say about the subject of land. What is said about land, while informed by historical criticism, is said theologically in a way that is to serve as a guideline for the current community of faith.[69] Katharine Doob Sakenfeld's volume, *Faithfulness in Action*, makes the same theological move—from the descriptive to the normative—and does so quite self-consciously.[70] Paul Hanson, after fourteen chapters about "The People Called," concludes with a final chapter on the implications of this material for the believing community.[71] If such moves are not within the domain of biblical theology's mandate, then a discipline needs to be created where such moves are legitimized and explored.

The practice by biblical theologians of bringing their work to bear on the current community does not necessarily make the argument that they should do so. However, these contemporary examples, not unlike the appeal for relevance by Rudolf Kittel and Paul Girgensohn in the 1920s, raise anew the question of the propriety of biblical theologians identifying the relevance of their work for the confessing community. This essay declares that it is appropriate.

A final comment, something of a footnote, is to observe that for biblical theologians to assume a norming role in theology is in keeping with an original vision for biblical theology. Biblical theology as a discipline is usually dated to 1787, the year in which J. P. Gabler in a formal lecture laid out the distinction between biblical theology and dogmatic theology. His vision for biblical theology was for it to be an historical discipline in contrast to dogmatic theology. He proposed that biblical theologians first describe with care what the "holy writers felt about divine matters." Such research would yield a "true" theology, namely one in accord with the biblical material. Next, the biblical theologian would collect the typical ideas of each biblical author and examine these in "comparison with the help of the universal notions."[72] This research would issue in "pure" theology. That program has only sporadically been followed through. Interpretations of what it means to do "pure" theology vary, but one must agree with Hayes/Prussner that in attempting "pure" theology, "the descriptive task moved to the level of the normative task.":[73]

The burden of this essay is not that the biblical theologians displace doctrinal theologians. The concern, highlighted by noting that historically biblical theologians have eschewed moving their conclusions upon the believing community in the form of truth claims, is that they now, for the reasons given, reverse their position. These reasons include a revised understanding of the function of theology as theory, a revised understanding of the relationship of biblical theology to systematic theology, considerations of what it means for biblical theology that its primary document is canon, and a critique of the older distinction between "meant" and "means." That distinction at one time reinforced the reluctance of biblical theologians to show how their work was to be appropriated by the community. But such reluctance cannot be justified.

Notes

1   R. N. Whybray, "Old Testament Theology—a Non-existent Beast?" in *Scripture: Meaning and Method. Essays Presented to Anthony Tyrell Hanson*, ed. B. P. Thompson (North Yorkshire: Pickering, 1987), 168-180.

2   John J. Collins, "Is a Critical Biblical Theology Possible?" in *The Hebrew Bible and Its Interpreters*, ed. W. H. Propp, Baruch Halpern, D. N. Freedman (Winona Lake, IN: Eisenbrauns, 1990), 14.

3   Ibid.. See also his "Biblical Theology and the History of Israelite Religion," in *Back to the Sources: Biblical and Near Eastern Studies*, ed. Kevin J. Rathcart and John J. Healey (Dublin: Glendale, 1989), 18.

4   James Barr, "The Theological Case Against Biblical Theology," in *Canon Theology, and Old Testament Interpretation*, ed. Gene Tucker, David Petersen, R. W. Wilson (Philadelphia: Fortress Press, 1988), 3-19.

5   Cited in W. A. Irwin, "The Reviving Theology of the Old Testament." *JR* 25 (1945): 246.

6   Reginald Fuller, in *Harpers Bible Dictionary*, s.v. "Theology, New Testament."

7   Quoted in James D. Smart, "The Death and Rebirth of Old Testament Theology," *JR* 23 (1943): 10.

8   W. A. Irwin, "The Reviving Theology of the Old Testament," *JR* 25 (1945): 244.

9   Jesper Høgenhaven, *Problems and Prospects of Old Testament Theology* (Sheffield: JSOT Press, 1988), 93; cf. H. G. Reventlow, "Zur Theologie des Alten Testaments," *TRu* 52 (1987): 221-67.

10   J. H. Hayes and Frederick Prussner, *Old Testament Theology: Its History and Development* (Atlanta: John Knox Press, 1985), 209.

11   Reginald Fuller, "New Testament Theology," in *The New Testament and Its Modern Interpreters*, ed. E. J. Epp and G. W. MacRae (Philadelphia: Fortress), 565.

12   Collins, "Biblical Theology and the History of Israelite Religion."

13   Cited in Irwin, "The Reviving Theology," 246.

14   Cf. Hayes and Prussner, *Old Testament Theology*, 153.

15 Otto Baab, *The Theology of the Old Testament* (Nashville: Abingdon-Cokesbury Press, 1949), 20.

16 Claus Westermann, "Aufgaben einer zukünftigen Biblischen Theologie," in *Erträge der Forschung am Alten Testament, Gesammelte Studien, 3* (München: Chr. Kaiser Verlag, 1984).

17 Brevard Childs, *Old Testament Theology in a Canonical Context* (Philadelphia: Fortress Press, 1985), 6.

18 Stendahl, *Meanings: The Bible as Document and as Guide* (Philadelphia: Fortress Press, 1984), 2. The essay was first published in 1962, in *IDB*, s.v. "Biblical Theology, Contemporary." in *IDB*; it appears in *Meanings* as "Biblical Theology: A Program," 11-44.

19 Walter Brueggemann, "Futures in Old Testament Theology," *HBT* 6 (1984): 1.

20 Kelsey, *The Usess of Scripture in Recent Theology* (Philadelphia: Fortress Press, 1975), 159, 161, 163, 166.

21 Ibid., 161.

22 Ben C. Ollenburger, "What Krister Stendahl 'Meant'—A Normative Critique of 'Descriptive Biblical Theology,'" *HBT* 8 (1986): 61-98. The following is largely a summary of Ollenburger's argument.

23 R. E. Clements, *Old Testament Theology* (Atlanta: John Knox Press, 1978), 11-15.

24 Collins, "Critical Biblical Theology?" 14.

25 Ollenburger, "What Stendahl 'Meant'," 90.

26 Rolf Knierim, "On the Task of Old Testament Theology," *HBT* 6 (1984): 94.

27 Irwin, "The Reviving Theology," 243.

28 Gerhard Ebeling, "The Meaning of 'Biblical Theology'," in *Word and Faith* (Philadelphia: Fortress Press, 1963), 89.

29 "'Whare', 'reine' oder 'neue' Biblische Theologie? Einige Anfragen zur neueren Diskussion um 'Biblische Theologie'," *JBT* 1 (1986): 141 (translation mine).

30 Fuller, "New Testament Theology," 577.

31 Stendahl, "Biblical Theology, Contemporary," 427-28.

32 Lews S. Ford, *The Lure of God: A Biblical Background for Process Theism* (Philadelphia: Fortress Press, 1978).

33 Thomas Finger is an example. See his *Christian Faith: An Escatological Approach*, 2 vols. (Scottdale: Herald Press, 1987, 1989).

34 Hayes and Prussner, *Old Testament Theology*, 209.

35 *The Theology of the Old Testament* (Abingdon-Cokesbury Press, 1949), 19; Hayes and Prussner, *Old Testament Theology*, 209. Th. C. Vriezen says something similar, in *An Outline of Old Testament Theology* (Oxford: Blackwell, 1948), 118-25.

36 Baab, *Theology of the Old Testament*, 19.

37   Irwin, "The Reviving Theology," 244.

38   Collins, "Critical Biblical Theology?" 14.

39   Barr, "Case Against Biblical Theology," 10.

40   Paul Hanson, in *Harper's Bible Dictionary*, s.v. "Theology, Old Testament."

41   Thomas Finger, "Biblical and Systematic Theology: A Proposal for their Interaction Concretized by Reference to the Atonement," unpublished paper, 1986, 14. (A revised version of Finger's paper is published as chapter 1 of this volume—ed.).

42   Barr, "Case Against Biblical Theology," 13.

43   Ibid., 14.

44   See Ollenburger, "Biblical Theology: Situating the Discipline," in *Understanding the Word*, ed. J. T. Butler, E. W. Conrad, B. C. Ollenburger (Sheffield: JSOT Press, 1985), 51.

45   Stendahl, *Meanings*, 1.

46   Collins, "Critical Biblical Theoloyg?" 15.

47   Barr, "Case Against Biblical Theology," 10.

48   Ritschl, "Diskussion um 'Biblische Theology'," 140-41.

49   Langdon Gilkey, "The Roles of the 'Descriptive' or 'Historical' and of the 'Normative' in our Work," *Criterion* 20 (1981): 10.

50   Ibid.

51   Finger, *Christian Theology*, 1:51.

52   Ibid., 53-54.

53   Ernest Best, "Fashions in Exegesis: Ephesians 1:3," in *Scripture: Meaning and Method*, 79-91.

54   Knierim, "Task of Old Testament Theology."

55   Paul Hanson, *The Diversity of Scripture: A Theological Interpretation* (Philadelphia: Fortress Press, 1982); Dunn, *Unity and Diversity in the New Testament: An Inquiry into the Character of Earliest Christianity* (Philadelphia: Westminster Press, 1977).

56   John Goldingay, *Theological Diversity and the Authority of the Old Testament* (Grand Rapids: Wm. B. Eerdmans, 1987).

57   Gilkey, "The Roles," 13.

58   Finger, *Christian Theology*, 1:55-56.

59   Ibid., 54-55.

60   Brevard Childs, *Biblical Theology in Crisis* (Philadelphia: Westminster, 1970), 100.

61   Clements, *Old Testament Theology*, 24.

62   Walter Brueggemann, "Futures in Old Testament Theology," *HBT* 6 (1984): 3.

63   Ollenburger, "Biblical Theology."

64   Brueggemann, "Futures," 3-4.

65   *Meanings*, 2.

66   Goldingay, *Theological Diversity and Authority*, 111.

67   Walter Brueggemann, "A Shape for Old Testament Theology, II: Embrace of Pain," *CBQ* 47 (1985): 414.

68   Walter Brueggemann, "Some Reflections on the Search for a Biblical Theology," *HBT* 4 (1982): 9.

69   Walter Brueggemann, *The Land* (Philadelphia: Fortress Press, 1977).

70   K. D. Sakenfeld, *Faithfulness in Action: Loyalty in Biblical Perspective* (Philadelphia: Fortress Press, 1985).

71   Paul Hanson, *The People Called* (San Francisco: Harper & Row, 1986).

72   Hayes and Prussner, *Old Testament Theology*, 3; John Sandys-Wunsch and Laurence Eldredge, "J. P. Gabler and the Distinction Between Biblical and Dogmatic Theology: Translation, Commentary, and Discussion of His Originality," *SJT* 33 (1980): 141-42.

73   See Hayes and Prussner, *Old Testament Theology*, 63; Ollenburger, "Biblical Theology."

Chapter 3

Biblical and Systematic Theology as Functional Specialties: Their Distinction and Relation

A. James Reimer

I
The Basic Argument

Christian theology in general is reflection on the grounds, contents, and experience of the Christian faith. It is an activity that assumes the transcendent reality of God, God's self-revelation in Jesus Christ, and God's ongoing presence in the life of the church and the world as the unifying theme(s) running through the diversity of the church's foundational texts and historical events, and the manifold interpretations of those texts and events. To the extent that a scholar (whether biblical, historical, systematic-dogmatic or practical-pastoral) is engaged in this activity with these assumptions, to that degree she is engaged in Christian theology. Technically speaking, therefore, the prevalent distinction among biblical, historical, systematic, and practical theology, as though these were four different theologies, is false.

All Christian theologians are engaged in one set of interdependent tasks and the interpretation of a common collectyion of foundational texts, directed toward a common goal. They specialize in different areas for mainly practical reasons of skill, temperament, convenience, and so on. Biblical theology, for instance, is not a separate genre of theology (although it is often seen to be just that) set over against systematic theology, as though it alone were truly biblical and were unconcerned about coherence, unity, synthesis, systematization, mediation, or even dogma. If it is a form of Christian theology, it is interested in these things. All theology is to a greater or lesser degree systematic, and all theology if it is Christian ought to be biblical. With these provisos, however, there is some value in differentiating among the areas of specialization (sometimes called "functional specialties")—biblical, historical, systematic, and practical—as long as we remember that, if their respective practitioners want to attach the common noun "theology" to their specialty, they are admitting to being engaged in a common enterprise with the others—Christian theology.

The primary focus of *systematic theology*, as a functional specialty, is the church within the world of contemporary culture—its language, values, assumptions, and demands. Its task is to summarize and schematize the essential tenets of the Christian faith, as revealed in Scripture and interpreted historically, for the purpose of helping the church to shape the beliefs and values of her adherents; to mediate between the world of the Bible and her life within contemporary culture; and critically to address the assumptions and demands of the present age, as well as her own ideological distortions. The primary focus of *biblical theology*, as a functional specialty, is the world of Scripture; that is, to research, analyze, synthesize, elucidate, interpret, and translate the biblical texts, and to identify the assumptions of the biblical age, using all the tools of modern culture and insights from tradition in order to do so. Both are essential to the life of the church. Biblical theology, with its greater concentration on the inner diversities and infrastructure of the biblical materials themselves, including the milieu of those writings, has the responsibility toward systematic (or dogmatic) theology of keeping it from ideologically falsifying the biblical texts (and world) in its necessary task of summarizing. Systematic theology, with its greater concentration on the assumptions of the contemporary world and the *summarized unities* of the tradition, has the responsibility toward biblical theology of identifying and unmasking the contemporary presuppositions that are inescapably present in, and may distort, biblical studies—for example, the positivistic fragmentation and quantification of Scripture.

I I
The Importance of Catechesis

The divisions and specializations within the general field of Christian theology are fluid, and they vary significantly from one historical period to another, from tradition to tradition, from institution to institution, and from scholar to scholar.[1] This fluidity suggests that these various schemas are relative, and developed to meet the exigencies of particular situations. One may lament this increasing differentiation as a fragmentation of what once was and ought still to be one basic, unified set of activities—the reading, interpretation, appropriation, and application of Scripture. Nevertheless, the specializations seem to be here to stay; they have to do with the accumulation of data that need to be absorbed but cannot be mastered by any one group of scholars, let alone by an individual. A division of labor between individuals, but also between groups of specialists, appears to be an unhappy necessity.

The most common and perhaps the most useful contemporary curricular categories are those dividing Christian theology into biblical, historical, systematic, and pastoral (or practical) specialties. I intend in this paper to concentrate on two of these commonly accepted disciplines—biblical "theology" and systematic "theology." I will attempt to delineate what I consider to be the distinctive operations and methodologies of each, at least functionally, in the present situation, giving special attention to systematic theology and its relation to biblical theology.

Leaving aside the thorny issue of whether or not the practitioners of biblical and systematic theology can properly fulfill their functions outside the community of faith, I will assume in this essay that in both cases the theologians belong existentially to a believing community of Christians (that is, they have experienced conversion, in some sense of that term[2]) and are seeking to be faithful in proclaiming the Christian understanding of God in and to the present age. They are, in short, engaged in a common enterprise— *theology.* Neither biblical nor systematic theology is antiquarian, interested in the past for its own sake. Each views its respective task as a form of piety and fidelity to God in the contemporary context.

The German-English *Catechism* that first initiated me into the life of the Altona Bergthaler Mennonite Church,[3] and which first introduced me to the 'systematic' categories of creation, fall, and redemption, began with the following question: "Was ist das Notwendigste, wonach ein Mensch in diesem Leben trachten soll?" The answer: "In Gottes Gemeinschaft und Gnade zu leben und nachmals die ewige Seligkeit zu erlangen." There followed a rather questionable translation. Question: "What should be our chief aim in this life?" Answer: To live in God's fellowship, enjoy his favor, and obtain eternal happiness hereafter." Despite the weak translation, and all of the modern Enlightenment and post-modern problems associated with this answer, I hold this affirmation to be fundamentally true and applicable to all Christians, including professional theologians. The alpha and omega of our theological work and reflection is to live in God's fellowship and grace, and to proclaim the same to others in our pluarlistic context.

This catechism summarized what its writers considered to be the essentials of the Christian faith, for the purpose of educating baptismal candidates; I consider this to be one of the essential tasks of systematic theology. The opening statement of the "Foreword" says: "This catechism was first published in the year 1783, at Elbing, Prussia, with the purpose of presenting to the Mennonite young people the cardinal truths of Christianity in a brief and simple form."[4] This catechetical manual characterizes itself as giving "Brief lessons from the Holy Scriptures;" it consists of 202 questions and answers, each supported by one or more Bible verses, divided into these major sections: Introduction; "Part One: The Creation" (ranging from God as Creator of all things, the Trinity, to God as preserver and ruler of the world); "Part Two: the Fall of Man" (dealing with the condition of humanity before, during, and after the Fall); "Part Three: The Redemption of Man" (covering the promise of redemption, the role of law, Christ and his death, resurrection, ascension, the Holy Spirit, faith, regeneration, justification, sanctification, the church, baptism, the Lord's supper, nonresistance, government and the oath, the future destiny of humanity, judgment, and so on).

What is going on here? For one thing, from the perspective of modern contextual-critical biblical scholarship, this catechism commits the unpardonable sin: it assumes without question an underlying canonical unity, ranges freely backwards and forwards across the Old and New Testaments, moves with ease from one book to another, and uncritically selects isolated Bible verses in support of its particular doctrinal framework—without ever asking any social-historical and contextual questions, admitting of any genuine heterogeneity in the biblical materials, or allowing for any hermeneutical difficulties. An yet, it seems to me that this catechism engages in a legitimate task and, in its own distinctive way, does what the Christian church has done from antiquity until recently; namely, it simplifies, summarizes, and schematizes what it believes to be true, for the purpose of shaping and nurturing the beliefs and values of the church's existing or potential adherents.

Whatever the strengths and weaknesses of George A. Lindbeck's "cultural-linguistic approach to religion and . . . regulative view of doctrine," a subject I will return to in the last part of this paper, I do think he helps us understand sympathetically what is going on in a catechism like this.[5] For one thing, Lindbeck's analysis lends support to my own long-standing contention that doctrinal language is indispensable for the Christian church, including the Mennonite church. I might add, here, that I consider confession, doctrine, creed, and dogma to be family members of the same literary and theological genre, even though there are important differences between them. Doctrinal formulations, while not the whole of it, are an intrinsic part of systematic theology's work. They represent the Christian community's attempt to develop a coherent picture out of the many diverse concepts, images, and symbols found in early Christian writings—particularly in reference to God, Jesus Christ, and the Holy Spirit—for the purpose of catechesis.[6]

Lindbeck is right in arguing that, historically, catechesis rather than translation "has been the primary way of transmitting the faith and winning converts for most religions down through the centuries."[7] In my view, this has also been an important aspect of the Mennonite way. Whether Lindbeck's postliberal cultural-linguistic model is the best way to conceive of doctrine or catechesis is another question. This point I want to make here is that Lindbeck is justified in stressing the importance of doctrine and catechesis in the life of religious communities and in the work of systematic theology—which, incidentally, he refers to as a 'descriptive' discipline: "The task of descriptive (dogmatic or systematic) theology is to give a normative explication of the meaning a religion has for its adherents."[8] For Lindbeck there is no such thing as "creedless Christianity." Doctrines, at least operationally if not officially, are a requisite for communal identity: "A religious body cannot exist as a recognizable collectivity unless it has some beliefs and/or practices by which it can be identified."[9]

Lindbeck is also clearly right in asserting repeatedly that the modern age and its theology have an antipathy to catechetical-doctrinal thinking and a concomitant dogmatic-systematic theology. This so for a number of reasons. First, doctrines in the narrow sense (meaning those central beliefs considered essential and normative for the existence of a particular religious community), and dogmatic theology in the broader sense (the explanation, interpretation, and justification of those doctrines), presuppose the existence of an organic religious community. However, the modern age is characterized precisely by the breakdown of community and community norms, as sociologists have been at such pains to point out. This disintegration of a cohesive communal society, or communal enclaves, is the consequence of modern notions of individual freedom and autonomous authenticity. What we have, in fact, is an increasingly global-homogeneous society in which only a privatized and interiorized religiosity appears able to survive. The experiential-expressive approach to religion—the liberal alternative to what Lindbeck somewhat problematically calls the classical "propositional" approach[10]—is more attractive to a culture defined by "religious privatism" and subjectivism."[11] The prevalent aversion to dogmatic standards reflects a theology inclined to accommodate and legitimate, rather than to stand over against, a pluralistic-atomistic age.

However, this contemporary resistance to doctrinal norms cannot be attributed simply to the perversity of modern culture. Lindbeck correctly perceives some conceptual difficulties with traditional doctrinal propositionalism. It cannot account for the development of doctrine over time, it is unable adequately to distinguish between what is essential and what is nonessential when interpreting doctrines in new situations, and it cannot deal satisfactorily with ecumenical issues.[12] In another context I have pointed out that in Mennonite churches—I believe this could be said about other traditions as well—various other ways of speaking about the Christian faith in the present situation have replaced the doctrinal-dogmatic approach, the therapeutic and socio-political models being two of the most obvious.[13] It is doubtful that these alternatives substantially improve upon the doctrinal-confessional genre. An understanding of the nature of doctrine and dogmatic theology is required that can meet some of these objections. To what extent Lindbeck's own cultural-linguistic approach meets these requirements remains to be discussed later. Here I simply wanted to introduce catechesis or doctrinal thinking as an essential aspect of systematic theology, and of theology in general, and as a way of distinguishing systematic from biblical theology.

I make no claims for originality here but am simply defending what I consider to have been an ancient understanding of the task of Christian theology. My own view is in fact very close to that of Karl Barth, for whom "Christian doctrine is the attempt, undertaken as a responsibility of the church, to summarize the gospel of Jesus Christ, as the content of the church's preaching. Its source and its goal is the authentic witness to the gospel in Holy Scripture."[14] For Barth, dogmatics is a critical, human science, located halfway between exegesis and practical theology, a means for testing the church's teaching and preaching; "not an arbitrary testing from a freely chosen standpoint," but a measuring of "the Church's proclamation by the standard of the Holy Scriptures, of the Old and New Testaments. Holy Scripture is the document of the basis, of the innermost life of the Church, the document of the manifestation of the Word of God in the person of Jesus Christ."[15] Dogmatics has not fallen from heaven. It is a "human and earthly" science by which the "Church draws up its reckoning in accordance with the state of its knowledge at different times." Thus, "Christian dogmatics will always be a thinking, an investigation and an exposition which are relative and liable to error."[16]

What is noteworthy is how high a regard Barth does have for the dogmatic formulations of the patristic period of the church, particularly the development of the classical trinitarian and christological dogmas, and the relative authority he is willing to assign them.[17] "Holy Scripture and the Confessions do not stand on the same level," he says. "We do not have to respect the Bible and tradition with like reverence and love, not even tradition in its most dignified manifestations." Nevertheless, confessions do have a certain kind of normativity: "If Holy Scripture has binding authority, we cannot say the same of the confessions. Yet there is still a nonbinding authority, which must be taken seriously."[18] For Barth, then, 'dogma' is simply the term we give to that which we in the church, and based on Holy Scripture, consider to be normative or valid in the church's proclamation and life. While this is the proper sphere of systematic or dogmatic theology, to the extent that biblical theology (or a biblical theologian) respects this normativity, to that extent it is in fact engaged in what I consider systematic-dogmatic theology.

III
Biblical Theology: Ollenburger versus Stendahl

In his provocative 1986 essay, "What Krister Stendahl 'Meant'—A Normative Critique of 'Descriptive Biblical Theology,'" Ben C. Ollenburger persuasively points out the logical and semantic confusions inherent in Stendahl's classic program for "biblical theology."[19] In his famous 1962 essay, "Biblical Theology, Contemporary," an article that significantly shaped the way biblical theologians understood their task thereafter, Stendahl proposed that biblical theology be limited to *describing* what the biblical texts *meant*, whereas systematic theology should be left with the *normative* task of *interpreting* what the texts *mean*.[20] Unfortunately, although Ollenburger hints at how biblical and systematic theology might differ from each other, he deliberately restricts himself to dismantling Stendahl's proposal and does not make any constructive proposal of his own. He succeeds in undermining the usefulness of Stendahl's underlying distinctions concerning the differences between biblical theology and systematic theology.

First, Ollenburger maintains that Stendahl's division between "'the descriptive study of the actual theology and theologies to be found in the Bible [biblical theology]','" and "'any attempt at a normative and systematic theology which could be called "biblical",'" in the end leaves biblical theologians with little more than historical studies—that is, studying the *"meanings* ascribed to the text by interpreters over history," without any means of adjudicating between alternative meaning statements.[21] For Stendahl, hermeneutics (the attempt to find the normative meaning of a given text) would appear, consequently, to belong solely to the domain of systematic theologians. Hermeneutical decisions, according to Stendahl, do not naturally grow out of the text itself but are made from a "specific theological stance," a stance that presupposes a community of faith and canonicity. In short, Stendahl, in Ollenburger's eyes, reduces all biblical studies to two types— historical (the realm of non-normative description) and normative systematic theology. Stendahl—so argues Ollenburger—gives us no clear method of relating the one to the other, of methodologically moving from description to normative work. By inference, one can assume here that Ollenburger thinks of biblical theology itself as being a transitional method or "discipline" standing halfway between history and systematic theology. I think Stendahl does in fact provide us with what he considers to be a connecting link between descriptive and normative statements, a bridge that grows out of historical description itself. It is this, in fact, which colors Stendahl's whole view of what systematic theology should be. But I'm getting ahead of myself.

Second, Ollenburger claims that the distinction between "descriptive" and "normative," which lies at the basis of Stendahl's whole argument, entails a logical and semantic confusion. For one thing, there is no reason why something cannot be both descriptive and normative at the same time. It is possible to have 'normative description.' Dogmatics, in the Barthian sense, for instance, claims to be both descriptive and normative. Further, normativity can mean different things: (a) it can mean 'to be constrained by a given set of rules or standards,' or (b) it can refer to 'a set of rules by which something else is to be constrained."[22] Thus, biblical theologians, for the most part, consider descriptions governed by the rules of the historical-critical method as normative in trying to understand texts. Stendahl assumes much too narrow a definition of normativity, taking it to refer to those accounts that are considered binding or authoritative by rules other than the historical-critical ones. Stendahl thinks that "Normative interpretations (accounts) of Scripture are to be understood as those interpretations by which we are constrained to order our beliefs and actions as Jews and Christians."[23] Ollenburger allows that "there is nothing at all wrong with this tendency . . ; it merely shows that descriptions can be offered of different things." The point that Ollenburger wants to make is that "'normative' accounts are not less descriptive than, say, strictly historical ones, and, on the other hand, strictly historical accounts are no less normative than these."[24] Ollenburger's agenda appears to be quite a modest one—namely, to demonstrate that even in its use of what is ordinarily considered to be a purely descriptive method, historical-criticism, biblical theology is making normative judgments. This is an extremely significant point, for it means that all biblical-theological work, including even its most descriptive tasks, is colored by *philosophical* presuppositions.

What is important here is not that historical description can also, and often does, make normative judgments (that to make normative descriptions is logically possible), but rather that historical descriptions necessarily entail normative presuppositions; and that in so doing, they have a philosophical (or systematic) side to them. The strength of Stendahl's argument is that he correctly identifies the "normativity" issue with systematics (or philosophy). The problem is that he separates description and normativity into two distinct disciplines. Ollenburger's essay in fact demonstrates that biblical theology is much more systematic (or philosophical) than it sometimes likes to think of itself as being. What Ollenburger does not address, unfortunately, is in what sense the descriptive-normative components of biblical theology might differ from those of systematic theology—or, for that matter, whether there is a rationale at all for their separate existence as disciplines within Christian theology.

Finally, in Ollenburger's opinion Stendahl's problems are simply compounded when he goes on to further differentiate biblical and systematic theology on the basis of the meant/means distinction. The problem with this dichotomy becomes evident as soon as one seeks a criterion by which to determine the property of a text (meant) apart from its interpretation (means). As Ollenburger convincingly shows, first by way of an inserted discussion of Samuel Terrien's problematic understanding of biblical theology, and then by a feat of complicated "symbolic logic," any attempt to describe what a biblical text meant apart from what it means involves one in the logical oddity of asserting that a simple entity T (Text) possesses two exclusive properties: M (Meant) and M' (Means), one capable of being described without reference to the other. The upshot of all this, for Ollenburger, is that to say something about what a text meant is invariably also to say something about what it means, and that biblical theologians are always engaged in both.

The fundamental problem with Ollenburger's essay, despite its obvious strengths as outlined above, is that it does not tell us when biblical theology (which Ollenburger evidently assumes to be a legitimate discipline in its own right) is doing historical work and when it is engaged in theology. He appears to be drawing an invisible line between "biblical theology as history" and "biblical theology as theology," without ever identifying how they are different. In fact, at some points he seems to imply that Stendahl's distinctions do after all apply to one but not to the other. Here is what Ollenburger says:

> That biblical theologians describe texts (or their theologies)
> and determine what they meant is of little use in differenti-
> ating biblical scholarship from other historical disciplines,
> or in distinguishing biblical theology from other kinds of
> biblical scholarship. But this characterization has proven

extremely useful in differentiating biblical scholarship
from theological inquiry generally, and for preventing biblical scholarship, as a historical discipline, from being given
theological responsibilities that historical disciplines cannot
legitimately exercise. While it is not always recognized, it
seems to me that this is where Stendahl's real contribution
lies.[25]

What is Ollenburger saying here? Is Stendahl's proposal helpful in distinguishing between historical work and theological work or not? What is
"theological inquiry generally" as something incompatible with "biblical
scholarship, as a historical discipline?" Is biblical theology, then, not engaged
in theological inquiry in general? Is this to be left to the systematic
theologians? The only sense I can make out of these statements is that
Ollenburger is drawing a distinction between 'history' and 'theology' within
the discipline of biblical theology itself.

This becomes a little clearer later in the essay when Ollenburger says
that

Stendahl is right to distinguish between history and
theology, and to urge us to practice the kind of civility that
does not try to mount historical arguments that depend on
theological warrants. But to contrast descriptive and normative as he does is to confuse the issue by asking us to contrast
the descriptive component of one discipline with the
normative component of another.[26]

What appears to be going on here is an attempt by Ollenburger to make
"biblical theology" a self-sufficient discipline, with both a historical and a
theological component, but quite different from and independent of
"systematic (or dogmatic) theology." My contention is that, when conceived of
in this way—that is, as one part of a separate discipline known as biblical
theology, the other part being history—theology tends to be defined primarily
in terms of the historical-critical (if not historicist) paradigm. This is implicit, I
think, in Ollenburger's observation that

Stendahl seems to think theology tells us how we *ought* to
believe or *what* we ought to believe. In a sense, this is the
case—in the same sense that it is true that history tells us
how and what we ought to believe, only about different
things. In fact, theology describes Christian belief, or
Christian faith. It is, we might say, an account of the grounds
and content of Christian faith, and there are properly descriptive and properly revisionary such accounts.[27]

Ollenburger may not have intended as much, but he does appear here to
be suggesting that "history" and "theology" use the same methodology; it is
just in their subject matter that they differ. That is, biblical theologians ought
to see their normative task as similar to the way history makes normative

judgments. The strength of Ollenburger's essay—his main intent—is in show-ing how the biblical theologian (as historian) is never doing purely descriptive but always also normative work.

I read Stendahl's 1962 essay, as well as his 1984 introduction to a reprint of it, before reading Ollenburger's article. What struck me positively about Stendahl's differentiation between biblical theology and systematic theology, despite its weaknesses, was how seriously he tried to limit the scope of biblical theology in order (i) to preserve the integrity of the biblical texts and their world as distinct (or distant) from our world, and (ii) to make room for the legitimate and ongoing task of systematic theology. He was, in fact, very deliberately counteracting an anti-systematic prejudice and methodological imperialism among biblical theologians. He says so quite explicitly in his 1984 introduction:

> In restricting the primary role of the biblical scholar to the descriptive task, it was my intention to liberate the theologi-cal enterprise from what I perceived as `the imperialism of biblical scholars' in the field of theology. The more clearly one sees 'what is meant', the more obvious it becomes how impossible it is to live without the ever-ongoing work of systematic theology. Biblical categories stimulate and guide, but do not confine the task of contemporary theology be it in the academy or the churches, in seminars or in sermons.[28]

To adapt Kant's famous dictum, Stendahl was limiting biblical theology in order to make room for systematic theology.[29]

Whether or not he pulled it off is, of course, another question. Now, especially after reading Ollenburger's critique, it seems to me that Stendahl's strict distinction between description and prescription (or interpretation), espe-cially when divided according to disciplines, will not work. How should one differentiate, then, between biblical and systematic theology? I would like to propose, below, that before one can answer this question one must first be clear about the difference between history and theology, in terms of both method and content.

Contrary to Ollenburger's charge that he does not provide us with a means of moving from the one discipline (the descriptive) to the other (the interpretive and normative), Stendahl does in fact give us precisely what he considers to be the bridge between the two, namely, *history itself*. Even the biblical theologian can find an organic unity running through the diversity of the biblical texts, and that is the unity of "sacred history;" this is the unity *"which holds the material together in the Bible itself."*[30] Thus, in the words of Stendahl, "the thrust of an OT theology . . . is ultimately to establish how history is not only a stage upon which God displays his nature through his acts, but that the drama itself is one of history."[31] Thus there is to be found within the historical world of the biblical materials themselves, open to the non-normative methodology of description, that which leads naturally into the world of systematic theology if understood historically. This is what he says:

> The descriptive approach has led us far beyond a conglomeration of diverse ideas, the development of which we may be able to trace. We are now ushered right into a world of biblical thought that deserves the name "theology" just as much as do the thoughts of Augustine, Thomas, Calvin, and Schleiermacher. . . . The relation to the historical record is not any more one where systematic theology takes the raw material of nonsystematic data of revelation and gives it systematic structure and theological stature. . . . It is a relation between two highly developed types of theology: on the one hand, theologies of history, from which all statements about God, Christ, man, righteousness, and salvation derive their meaning and connotations, in terms of their function within the plan and on the plane of history; and on the other hand, theologies of an ontological sort, where Christianity is understood in terms of the nature of God, Christ, man, and so forth.[32]

It is not entirely clear, from this passage, whether or not Stendahl allows for the legitimate role of both types of theology, one historical and the other dogmatic. Neither is this clear from his other statements in the essay. However, it does seem that Stendahl, while not wanting to reject outright the 'ontological' approach to theology (or what he calls the "once for all" or "perfect tense" of biblical thought, as the Greeks thought of it), the overriding paradigm by which he wants to understand theological categories is the "radically historical" one. This historical model stands, for Stendahl, in direct contrast to the "radical, ahistorical" model of a Barth or a Bultmann.

I want to argue that, while theology must take history with great seriousness, as a discipline it must retain its own distinct methodology, which is quite different from the historical one in the assumptions it makes and in the way it deals with its subject matter. While both biblical and systematic theologians are accountable to the historian in some sense, both, to the degree that they are Christian theologians, make what I call ontological assumptions that the historian *as historian* cannot make. There is no doubt that the historian is both descriptive and normative, and may even make ontological assumptions; in fact, the historicist gives history itself ontological status. However, the Christian theologian cannot make history the primary ontological category. For her, I would argue, the underlying unifying assumption is a trinitarian one—the suprahistorical reality of God, God's self-disclosure *in history* (not *as history*), and God's ongoing presence historically in the life of the church and the world. These are not solely historical assertions. They are also ontological affirmations; that is, they purport to say something *theologically* (a nonliteralistic way of speaking and thinking about things) about the structure(s) of reality.

The historian as historian cannot make these assumptions methodologically determinative. I would like to suggest that the oft-perceived conflict between biblical theology and systematic theology is really a conflict within biblical theology itself. It cannot make up its methodological mind between history and theology. In naming itself "theology," it clearly commits itself to making assumptions and speaking a language that the historian as historian (including the biblical historian) cannot make or speak. The temptation for the biblical theologian is, therefore, either to disguise her extra-historical theological presuppositions and commitments as descriptive history, or not to be theological at all but positivist in her treatment of the Bible.

There is an important place for the biblical scholar as historian (with all of the historical presuppositions that are peculiar to the historian) in biblical studies. However, if there is such a discipline as "biblical theology," in adopting this terminology it *ipso facto* joins the methodological family of theology (of which systematic theology is also a member); in so doing, it acknowledges making theological assumptions about God, Jesus Christ, and history that the biblical scholar as historian cannot make. That the biblical theologian's specialized sphere of study is the biblical world itself does not change her underlying theological assumptions, which she has in common with the systematic theologian, and with which she approaches the biblical materials.

IV
Systematic Theology: What Is its Task?

I think it could be persuasively argued that "biblical theology" ought not be conceived, strictly speaking, as a separate discipline but rather as a functional specialty within theology in general, of which systematic theology is another specialty.[33] In order to help us differentiate between these two specialties it may be useful to look at the first few centuries of the Christian church.

During the patristic period there were two parallel movements going on side by side, more or less during the same period and basically for the same reasons: one was canonization and the other creedalization.[34] While it is true that socio-political forces were at work in both movements, both were nonetheless attempts by the early Christian community to establish norms by which to preserve the truth of the apostolic witness; or to put it negatively, they were attempts to guard against the heretical distortion of that truth. Further, both were theological developments beyond the earliest form and content of the witness. The selection process of canonization, whatever may have been its primary criteria, was in fact a narrowing for normative purposes. The process of creedal formulation was a more intensified narrowing for normative purposes. In short, creedalization was doing the same thing canonization was doing, except in summary form.

The importance (and strength) of the canonical writings over the confessional-creedal statements of the early church was that they preserved within themselves a much greater (although still selective) diversity of historical and theological materials and positions. The importance (and strength) of the confessional-creedal formulations was that they systematized the multiplicity of images, symbols, experiences, and accounts within the canonical writings—for (i) catechetical purposes and for (ii) apologetic purposes, both necessary in the church's missionary task.

Biblical theology and systematic theology are parallel theological activities and are related to each other somewhat as were the early church's parallel movements of canonization and creedalization. Biblical theology takes its cue from the one, systematic theology from the other. Both are essential to the life of the church in the world, and both have their particular strengths and dangers, for which each needs the compensating strengths of the other. Biblical theology has as its specialty the analysis, interpretation, and translation of the biblical texts,[35] using all the various critical tools and methodologies available to it (historical, literary, archaeological, sociological, and philosophical.[36] In its being theological, however, it is more than a scientific methodology and acknowledges a hermeneutical bias: it takes its subject matter to be the Word of God,[37] and, consequently, as having a normative (or canonical) claim over us. Systematic theology has as its specialty the summarizing and schematizing of the essential tenets of the Christian faith for the purpose of helping the church in shaping the beliefs and values of her adherents, mediating between the world of the Bible and her life within contemporary culture, and critically addressing the assumptions and demands of the present age. In this task, the concern for doctrinal formulations plays a vital role.

A recent example of the confessional-doctrinal imperative of Christian theology is the Barmen Confession. The point of division among Christians in the Third Reich was not solely between those who claimed fidelity to Scripture and those who did not. Both the German Christians (at least a significant number of them) and Confessing Christians based their positions on Scripture. In fact, some of the best biblical scholars sided with the German Christians. Good biblical scholarship in itself did not guarantee sound theology (let alone right politics). In this situation members of the Confessing Church found it necessary to summarize the essentials of the Christian truth, as they perceived it, in propositional form, clearly dividing between right belief and wrong belief. A confessional or doctrinal statement in itself does not guarantee good theology (or good politics), but it does recognize the need for articulating, as clearly as possible, what one believes to be true and how this applies in a given situation. The danger in such confessional-dogmatic narrowing, especially when it becomes a tool in the hands of a political power, is that other legitimate points of view are inevitably excluded. However, this danger does not cancel out the need for, or the legitimacy of, such doctrinal summarizing; it simply means that all such systematization and narrowing must be recognized for what it is—a finite human activity and language subject to error.

Confessional-doctrinal thinking is important to systematic theology not exclusively for its own sake but for three reasons: (i) to inculcate certain beliefs and values in the actual and potential adherents of the Christian church (catechesis); (ii) to mediate between the world of the Bible and the world of the church within contemporary culture; (iii) to address critically the assumptions and demands of contemporary culture. I have spoken to the first earlier in this paper. Let me conclude with a few observations concerning the second and third.

In another context I have argued that doctrines are really mediating principles or 'middle axioms' that bridge the world of Scripture and the contemporary situation, and are useful in dealing with new situations and new issues as they arise for the church.[38] In a recent article I have indicated how this might work when dealing with a specific issue like homosexuality from a theological perspective.[39] Although I take biblical theology to be interested in mediation as well (mediation and translation),[40] the kind of mediation that systematic theology is compelled and ready to undertake is more radical, it seems to me, than that of biblical theology. Systematic theology is prepared to move beyond the biblical texts quite deliberately and consciously in attempting to address contemporary issues that the biblical text itself does not adequately address. But it does this in a way continuous with or growing naturally out of the biblical materials. Its paradigm is the way the early ecumenical creeds, in addressing the trinitarian and christological issues, moved within and yet beyond the biblical writings. In other words, systematic theology does not simply translate, it mediates. But it does not do so through free association or unrestrained individual imagination. It follows certain formal guidelines, known as doctrines, which have their foundation in Scripture and have received their most universal articulation in the early ecumenical creeds. Thus, there is a kind of classical balance between formal restraint and creative imagination in the work of systematic theology.

The danger of such mediation is that one capitulates to the dominant assumptions of an age. It is incumbent upon biblical theology to provide a bulwark against a simple accommodation of the church's foundational writings to contemporary culture. Biblical theology's primary focus as a specialty is the world of Scripture; its interest in the language, assumptions, methodologies, and insights of contemporary culture is directed primarily toward the illumination of the Bible's world and the translation of that world into contemporary language. Thus, biblical theology jealously guards the distance between the biblical world and the contemporary world. The main focus of systematic theology is the contemporary situation, that is, the illumination of the church's life within contemporary culture from a Christian perspective. In this it is uniquely torn between what might be called a "prophetic-critical no" and a "priestly-sacramental yes" to the assumptions of the modern age.[41]

The triumph of technical-analytical reason in modern technology, with its accompanying view of reality, nature, and history, has its own metaphysics and ontology, which in my view are very difficult to reconcile with classical Christianity and God as transcendent creator, to whom human beings are accountable.[42] The privatization of religion that comes with the victory of a therapeutic understanding of human nature in modern post-communal culture, as manifested in the "cult of self worship," may be seen as a direct counterpart to the dominance of modern technique, and equally as irreconcilable with biblical Christianity.[43] These are just two examples of the assumptions of the modern age, which suggest that we are in fact becoming a much more globally homogeneous culture than a superficial analysis of modern diversity and pluralism would lead us to believe. It is these assumptions that systematic theologians need to address and critically analyze in the light of the Christian kerygma.

One of the strengths of George Lindbeck's "cultural-linguistic" approach to religion and his "rule theory" view of doctrine is the importance he places on foundational texts and "intratextual theology." In this model believers conform their experience to the Bible rather than the other way around. "Intratextual theology," he says, "redescribes reality within the scriptural framework rather than translating Scripture into extrascriptural categories. It is the text, so to speak, which absorbs the world, rather than the world the text."[44] Or to put it in other words, "To become a Christian involves [not so much making a decision as] learning the story of Israel and of Jesus well enough to interpret and experience oneself and one's world in its terms."[45] According to Lindbeck, the danger has always been that extrabiblical materials become the framework for biblical interpretation. This was the case in rationalism, pietism, and historical criticism, in which the biblical text became, not a lens through which one viewed the world, but an object of study through the lens of the external world.

The irony is that Lindbeck's whole model grows out of a very contemporary agenda—ecumenism. This is what he says:

> Although the focus of this book is on extra-Christian theological and ecumenical issues, the theory of religion and religious doctrine that it proposes is not specifically ecumenical, nor Christian, nor theological. It rather derives from philosophical and social-scientific approaches; and yet, so I shall argue, it has advantages, not only for the nontheological study of religion but also for Christian—and perhaps also non-Christian—ecumenical and theological purposes.[46]

I would suggest that Lindbeck's "cultural-linguistic" model is in some ways more faithful to recent linguistic theories like those of Noam Chomsky and

Ludwig Wittgenstein than it is to traditional understandings of Christian theology or doctrine. This is most clearly evident in his attempt to address the thorny issues of truth claims. According to Lindbeck, ". . . a religious utterance, one might say, acquires the propositional truth of ontological correspondence only insofar as it is a performance, an act or deed, which helps create that correspondence."[47] Further,

> Just as grammar by itself affirms nothing either true or
> false regarding the world in which language is used, but
> only about language, so theology and doctrine, to the extent
> that they are second-order activities, assert nothing true or
> false about God and his relation to creatures, but only
> speak about such assertions.[48]

This touches upon the fundamental problem with Lindbeck's model. How does one ultimately arbitrate between competing cultural-linguistic systems? It is well and good that, as Christians, we ought to shape our experience in accordance with the biblical stories and not in terms of propositional truth claims. I think Lindbeck is right to criticize wooden propositionalism with its particular correspondence theory of truth, although he fails to differentiate adequately between modern propositionalism and classical creedal thinking. The question remains: why one story over another, why one semiotic system over another? For Lindbeck, despite his admirable efforts to do so, there is ultimately no way of answering this question, because all criteria are internal to a particular cultural-linguistic framework. In the end, he is caught in hopeless cultural-linguistic relativism, a fate that haunts all of us. Where in Lindbeck's system is there the possibility of a radical breaking-in from the outside? Where is the basis for missions and conversion? It seems to me that in an age no longer defined by a variety of traditional cultural-linguistic systems but by one dominant, technological cultural-linguistic system, Lindbeck's proposal does not offer the radical critique of contemporary culture that is demanded from the systematic theologian.

The primary focus of systematic theology is the church within contemporary culture, and its task is to summarize the tradition (particularly its biblical moment) for the purposes of (i) catechesis and of (ii) mediation. However, in order for it to be able to do this comprehensively, systematic theology must understand and address the particular contemporary culture within which it finds itself—its language, art, philosophy, religions, politics, economics, and so on. Only as it listens to and understands these bearers of culture can it determine what within contemporary culture is authentic and positive (supportive of the created order) and what is negative (destructive of that order), in the light of the Christian revelation. Where Lindbeck's proposal is useful is in emphasizing the particular cultural-linguistic conditionedness of all our religious and theological feeling, thinking, and acting. However, it is not clear to me that his model allows for the radical breaking in, shattering, and judging of a particular cultural-linguistic context, or contemporary technological culture as a whole, from the outside.

Seen from a purely "profane" perspective, the crises of modern and postmodern culture—the injustices perpetrated by both western capitalist and eastern communist-socialist countries on minority groups, the grave moral perils arising out of medical advances and biogenetic experimentation, the objectification and destruction of nature brought about by the hubris of modern technology, the growing gap between rich and poor, both within our own societies and between first, second, and third world; the nuclear threat, not to mention the unimaginable atrocities of the past century—would appear to call for more universal, transcultural, and translinguistic answers than what Lindbeck's model offers. Seen from the Christian perspective, the underlying affirmations imbedded in the church's confessions, doctrines, creeds, and dogmas are more than "rules" intrinsic to a "language game;" they assert something fundamental (call it ontological, metaphysical, whatever you like) about God as transcendent reality, God as freely entering into and acting within history (paradigmatically in Jesus Christ), and God as ultimate author of human dignity and the dignity of the created order as a whole. These fundamental affirmations by the Christian church are conditioned but not exhausted by a cultural-linguistic-semiotic view of religion and theology. It is at the point of this claim—that Jesus Christ and the biblical witness to Jesus Christ is not simply one among a number of stories, not simply our story, but *the* story, the Word of God to us—that biblical theology and systematic theology become Christian theology.

Notes

1   For instance, Bernard Lonergan, to whom I am indebted for my notion of systematic theology as a functional speciality, divides theology into eight functional specialties: research, interpretation, history, dialectic, foundations, doctrines, systematics, and communications (*Method in Theology* [New York: Herder and Herder, 1972], 127).   David Tracy, strongly influenced by Lonergan, works with a tripartite scheme: fundamental theology, linked primarily to the public of the academy; systematic theology, linked primarily to the public of the church; and practical theology, focused primarily on society. "Theology, in fact," he says, "is a generic name not for a single discipline but for three: fundamental, systematic and practical theologies.   Each of these disciplines needs explicit criteria of adequacy" (*The Analogical Imagination* [New York: Crossroad Books, 1981], 3).   While most seminary programs divide their curriculums into biblical, historical, systematic, and practical (or pastoral) theology, some graduate theological programs experiment with different classifications; the Conrad Grebel Master of Theological Studies program has four subject areas: Scripture; theology and philosophy; history, society, culture; and ethics, mission, ministry.

2   My use of 'conversion' here is similar to that of Lonergan, who says "by conversion is understood a transformation of the subject and his world. Normally it is a prolonged process though its explicit acknowledgement may be concentrated in a few momentous judgments and decisions. Still it is not just a development or even a series of developments. Rather it is a resultant change of course and direction. . . . Conversion, as lived, affects all of a man's conscious and intentional operations. It directs his gaze, pervades his imagination, releases the symbols that penetrate to the depths of his psyche" (*Method in Theology*, 130-31).   I would argue that conversion—for Mennonites, theologically a condition of church membership—profoundly affects the way one goes about studying the Bible, church history, systematics and doctrine, and the practical life of the church.

3   *Catechism: German and English* (Altona: D. W. Friesen & Sons, 1954, 1957).

4   Ibid., 132.

5   George A. Lindbeck, *The Nature of Doctrine: Religion and Theology in a Postliberal Age* (Philadelphia: Westminster Press, 1984), 19.

6   Ibid., 94.

7   Ibid., 132.

8   Ibid., 113,

9   Ibid., p. 74.

10   His own, third option is a postliberal cultural-linguistic model. The problem with Lindbeck's schematization is that everything traditional—that is, everything premodern—is classified as "propositional," in contrast to modern (or nineteenth-century liberal) experientialism, and postmodern cultural linguisticism.   This is an unfair caricature of the ancients' understanding of theology. Lindbeck seems to recognize this when he says, quite correctly, "Both the Protestant who insists on scriptural inerrancy and the Roman Catholic traditionalist counterpart are likely to be suffering from vulgarized forms of a rationalism descended from Greek philosophy by way of a Cartesian and post-Cartesian rationalism reinforced by Newtonian science; but in the early centuries of the church, ontological truth by correspondence had not yet been limited to propositionalism.   Fundamentalist literalism, like experiential-expressivism, is a product of modernity" (ibid., 51). So is Lindbeck's own cultural-linguistic model a product of modernity, one might add. The point is, however, that while Lindbeck sometimes acknowledges that his so-called "traditional 'propositionalist'" category does not fit the ancients, he seems again and again to include the classical theological tradition under this category. I would suggest that classical theology, as represented by the church fathers during the classical period of orthodoxy, did not view doctrine either propositionally, in the fundamentalist mode; experientially, in the nineteenth-century liberal mode; or cultural-linguistically, in the postmodern mode; rather, they viewed it confessionally, with "propositional-ontological," "experiential-expressive," and "cultural-linguistic" components. Absolutely essential to the classical way of thinking and confessing was a trinitarian

understanding and experience of reality, making it both continuous and discontinuous with the Greco-Roman tradition, on the one hand, and the Hebraic world on the other. Charles Norris Cochrane's *Christianity and Classical Culture* (London: Oxford University Press, 1940) remains a classic on this topic.

11   Lindbeck, *The Nature of Doctrine*, 77-79.

12   Ibid., 78.

13   "Mennonite Theological Self-Understanding, the Crisis of Modern Anthropocentricity, and the Challenge of the Third Millennium," in *Mennonite Identity: Historical and Contemporary Perspectives*, ed. Calvin W. Redekop and Samuel J. Steiner (Lanham, MD: University Press of America, 1988), 13-38.

14   Karl Barth, *Learning Jesus Christ Through the Heidelberg Catechism* (Grand Rapids: Wm. B. Eerdmans, 1981), 17.

15   Karl Barth, *Dogmatics in Outline* (New York: Harper & Brothers, 1959), 12, 13.

16   Ibid., 10, 11.

17   Karl Barth, *Church Dogmatics*, vol. 1:1 (Edinburgh: T. & T. Clark, 1936), 431-40.

18   Barth, *Outline*, 13.

19   Ben C. Ollenburger, "What Krister Stendahl 'Meant'—A Normative Critique of 'Descriptive Biblical Theology,'" *HBT* 8 (1986): 61-98.

20   Krister Stendahl, "Biblical Theology: A Program," in *Meanings: The Bible as Document and as Guide* (Philadelphia: Fortress Press, 1984), 11-44. The essay was first published in 1962, in *IDB*, s.v. "Biblical Theology, Contemporary." My own reading was based on the 1984 reprint. Ollenburger bases his critique on Stendahl's 1965 article, "Methodology in the Study of Biblical Theology, in *The Bible in Modern Scholarship*, ed. J. P. Hyatt (Nashville: Abingdon, 1965), 196-209.

21   Ollenburger, "What Stendahl 'Meant'," 69.

22   Ibid., 74.

23   Ibid., 77.

24   Ibid.,

25   Ibid., 61-62.

26   Ibid., 78.

27   Ibid.

28   Stendahl, "Meanings," in *Meanings: The Bible as Document and as Guide*, 1.

29   Immanuel Kant: "I have therefore found it necessary to deny knowledge in order to make room for faith (*Critique of Pure Reason*, trans. Norman Kemp Smith (Toronto: Macmillan, 1929), 29.

30   Stendahl, "Biblical Theology: A Propopsal," 29 (emphasis his).

31   Ibid., 25.

32   Ibid., 30.

33   This depends, of course, on how loosely one defines what constitutes a 'discipline'. David Tracy, for example, goes into an extensive discussion of theology as a legitimate academic discipline with certain criteria of adequacy, warrants, and backing (or publicness), like every other university discipline. Actually, Tracy argues against the view that theology, generically speaking, is one separate discipline, and maintains that theology consists of three disciplines—fundamental, systematic, and practical—each making its own truth and meaning claims, and needing separate criteria of adequacy (*The Analogical Imagination*, 14-31). It is not clear where, in Tracy's whole scheme of things, biblical theology or biblical studies fits as a separate focus; it appears to belong most comfortably in his discipline of systematic theology. I am more inclined than is Tracy to give 'biblical theology' a distinct place in the theological enterprise, but to argue for the generic methodological unity of all types of theological studies, whether biblical, historical, systematic, or practical. To define 'biblical theology' and 'systematic theology' as distinct disciplines, with separate methodologies and separate criteria of adequacy, strikes me as undermining the unity of Christian theology itself. That is why Lonergan's notion of distinct but interdependent "functional specialties," within theology as a unified method, appeals to me.

34   I am not suggesting here that the Bible and the creeds have equal authority for the Christian church, merely that the selection of the biblical writings and the defining of orthodoxy in the creeds took place more or less during the same time (creedalization extending temporally beyond canonization) and for similar reasons. The apostolic witness to Christ as recorded in the biblical writings themselves is prior (in both authority and chronology) to the formulation of the creeds. It could be argued, on the other hand, that the confession-content of the creeds (e.g., Jesus is Lord) reaches farther back than does most of the written content of the biblical materials themselves, and that it is, thus, more primal or primary.

35   I am using the term 'translation' deliberately here, to describe the work of the biblical theologian in contrast to 'mediation' as the work of the systematic theologian. Translation is what a biblical scholar like Paul Minear is doing when he is preparing a new *Revised Standard Version* of the Bible. His primary goal is to present the original as accurately as possible. Because the meaning of words and concepts change, he needs to make changes here and there; he tries, for instance, to use more inclusive language wherever the original warrants it. The biblical theologian does more than simply translate, she also elucidates, interprets, analyzes, and synthesizes, enters into and engages herself with the assumptions of the biblical world. Nevertheless, I think the work of the Bible translator is a kind of paradigm for what the biblical theologian does or ought to do—focus on the world of the Bible, and present that world as faithfully as possible to us in our world. At the point where the biblical theologian begins consciously to move beyond the biblical world in order to 'mediate' or 'bridge' these two worlds, the line between the task of biblical and systematic theology becomes more fuzzy.

36   In the words of Raymond B. Williams, "Thus, the Bible is not a captive of one methodology; rather, literary, historical, sociological, archeological, and philosophical analyses complement the study of the Bible. Genealogical relationships of disciplines and methods exist so that the study of the bible assumes an inter-disciplinary character. Thus, the student of the Bible applies a wide range of critical methods developed in the Western intellectual tradition to the central text of that tradition" ("Foreword," in *The Bible and the Liberal Arts* [Crawfordsville, IN: Wabash College, 1986). The point is that all these different methodologies are devoted to the study of the biblical texts themselves. The systematician also is an interdisciplinarian, but is more directly engaged in conversing with and addressing the various disciplines as bearers of the assumptions of contemporary culture, intent both on mediation and on confrontation.

37   It is at the point of this faith bias that the biblical theologian and the systematic theologian are united in their methodologies. It is here that both of them are Christian theologians.

38   A. James Reimer, "Mennonite Theological Self-Understanding."

39   "A Call for Compassion and Moral Rigour," *Mennonite Reporter* 17, 13 (June 22, 1987): 7-9.

40   Because the biblical theologian is not simply a historian but also a theologian—that is, she considers the biblical writings to have authority and normativity as the 'Word of God' for herself and for the Christian community—the primary motive for specializing in the biblical texts and the biblical world is to discover in what sense that world has authority over us, and how it can be made accessible to the believing community. Here again, the biblical theologian and the systematic theologian overlap in their specialties.

41   Culture (e.g., language, art, science, politics, economics, and so on) is that which makes us human. One cannot throw off culture without losing one's humanity. Contemporary culture (whether one views it on the superficial level of its diversity or on the deeper level of its homogeneity) is the culture within which our own humanity is being expressed; it is a culture from which we cannot extricate ourselves. There are, of course, both positive (divine?) and negative (demonic?) elements in every culture. It is the task of systematic theology to analyze modern culture and to determine which aspects are to be affirmed (as those which are supportive of our own humanity and universal humanity) and which are to be rejected (as destructive of humanity). For the Christian, of course, what it means to be human receives its primary definition from God's Word in Jesus Christ.

42   The uniqueness of modern technology and the assumptions behind it—particularly its presuppositions concerning human freedom, the domination of human and nonhuman nature, the reduction of reason to technical or analytical reason, and its homogenizing effect on modern world culture—find their most penetrating articulation in the writings of Martin Heidegger, Hans Jonas, George Grant, and Jacques Ellul, among others. At the very heart of modern

technology, it would appear, is a denial of any accountability to a transcendent reality.

43   Cf. Philip Rieff, *The Triumph of the Therapeutic: Uses of Faith After Freud* (Chicago: University of Chicago Press, 1966, 1987); Paul C. Vitz, *Psychology As Religion: The Cult of Self-worship* (Grand Rapids: Wm. B. Eerdmans, 1977).

44   *Nature of Doctrine*, 118.

45   Ibid., 34.

46   Ibid., 7-8.

47   Ibid., 65. To Lindbeck's credit, he seriously addresses the problem of truth claims, and admits that the great advantage of the cognitive-propositional view of religion (in contrast with the experiential-expressive view) is that it can allow for such truth claims, and that it is the burden of the cultural-linguistic approach to show that it also can do so. But despite his valiant attempts to demonstrate that it can, through his intrasystematic notion of truth, and even a certain kind of propositional-correspondence view of truth (in which the entire system can be described as a giant proposition corresponding to what it considers to be "Most Important," and "Ultimately Real"), the truth is in the end still described in terms of practice—living out one's story. The question that remains is this: Is there such a thing as a wrong story, or are there right and wrong parts to a story, and how (by what criteria) does one determine when a story is right and when it is wrong?

48   Ibid., 69.

Chapter 4

Critical Theology and the Bible:
A Response to A. James Reimer

Gordon D. Kaufman

First I want to sketch briefly what I take to be Jim Reimer's position; then I shall pose some questions for further discussion.

Reimer's position on the relationship of biblical and systematic theology stems directly from his conception of theology itself. I will come back to the significance of this point, below. For now we will simply note that he views both of these disciplines (or emphases) as functional differentiations or specializations within theology. In this respect, for Reimer biblical theology is to be sharply distinguished from strictly *historical* work on the Bible; the latter does not normally make theological assumptions but only historical ones. Reimer does *not* really give a clear argument for the conception of Christian theology itself that he is using here, a conception on which everything else depends. He simply affirms what he later calls a "doctrinal-confessional" understanding (p. 41), and he seems to think it is more or less self-evident that this is the only justifiable view. For this conception there appear to be two fundamental features of Christian theology: (a) theology must be "biblical," and (b) it must be concerned with the situation and task of "the church within the world of contemporary culture" (p. 50). These two features provide theology's two principal *foci*, and they thus determine the understanding of the relationships between biblical and systematic theology. These two are simply *functional* distinctions within Christian theology itself, which is a single comprehensive discipline with four sub-disciplines—the other two being historical theology and practical theology.

According to Reimer, biblical theology focuses on and sets out an interpretation of biblical texts and ideas (using all the tools of modern scholarship), but it must do so, of course, with an eye on the problems and tasks of the church in the modern world; thus, it is not simply a kind of positivistic or uncommitted historical work. Systematic theology focuses on the situation of the church within the modern world—its language, values, assumptions, demands, etc.—attempting to summarize and schematize "essential tenets of the Christian faith, as revealed in Scripture and interpreted historically" (p. 38).

59

So biblical and systematic theology represent two interdependent poles or emphases in the one common theological task. Biblical theology has the special responsibility "to provide a bulwark against a simple accommodation of the church's foundational writings to contemporary culture" (p. 50). Systematic theology mediates biblical materials to the modern situation of the church by means of its doctrinal formulations. Each task is indispensable; and it is important for those who take up either to keep in mind the other with which their work is intrinsically interconnected.

This bi-polar conception of theology seems at first glance to be relatively clear and straightforward. However, I want to suggest that there are some deep problems lying beneath the surface, problems that need considerable further discussion. I will take up three issues.

A. *The Problem of Construing Scripture*

Reimer suggests that, although systematic theology "must move beyond the biblical text quite deliberately and consciously in attempting to address contemporary issues that the biblical text itself does not adequately address" (p. 50), it does so "in a way continuous with or growing naturally out of the biblical materials" themselves (p. 50). This notion of a simple or "natural" or straightforward relationship between biblical and systematic theology conceals some difficult problems. David Kelsey's work some years ago (*The Uses of Scripture in Recent Theology* [Philadelphia: Fortress Press, 1975], not mentioned by Reimer) showed that there is no such thing as a "continuous" or "natural" development of doctrine out of scripture. Scripture itself must be "construed" (Kelsey's term) as some particular sort of literature that we use for certain purposes; and such a construal always involves an imaginative act of the theologian. *How* Scripture is to be construed is not directly given by Scripture itself, and this accounts for its construal in many different ways by different Christian theologians—as history, story, sets of beliefs or truths, the praise of God, a vehicle for existential self-understanding, the presentation of a kerygma, etc. Scripture is, in fact, much too pluralistic in character to interpret itself, and it is capable of being put to many different uses and understandings. Thus, Scripture cannot clearly authorize any one particular way of construing it. Many different sorts of construals of Scripture can each claim some plausibility, and they lead, thus, to many different sorts of theology. So even if we grant Reimer's point—that biblical theology and systematic theology are two interdependent poles—this in fact tells us very little about how these poles are actually related to each other, or how they ought to be related to each other. The really difficult problems remain unaddressed. I would like to hear a good bit more about how Reimer understands the movement *from* Scripture *to* theology.

B. *The Problem of a Doctrine of Scripture*

It should be clear from what I have just said that Scripture itself does not and cannot determine the actual relationship of Scripture to theology. There is no specifically *scriptural* idea or doctrine of this relationship; indeed, there is no scriptural idea of *theology* (of the sort Reimer is proposing to practice) at all. Thus, the *biblical theology* pole cannot determine the relationship between biblical theology and systematic theology. We are left, then, with two alternatives: Either (a) this question of how this relationship and interconnection is defined and justified will be left unaddressed and unexamined, and one will simply follow out some traditional patterns of thought rather uncritically; or (b), it will be through *theological reflection* itself that the question of the proper meaning and use of Scripture—and thus the understanding of the relationship of Scripture to theology—is explored and is to be answered. In Reimer's paper, I am sorry to say, it appears that the first of these two alternatives is accepted. There is no carefully argued theological discussion of the nature of Scripture; of the question of biblical authority (what *is* this? how does it work?); of the respects in which the Bible is authoritative and the respects in which it is not; of the variety of literary genres and documents in the Bible, etc. All of these questions, Reimer seems to take for granted, are unimportant for the problem of the relationship of biblical to systematic theology—or they are taken to have self-evident answers: Scripture is simply the "foundation" for all theological doctrines (p. 50), and the fundamental binding "authority" and "norm" for all theological work (p. 42).

We really need an explicit theological *doctrine of Scripture*—that is, we need to move to the second of the two alternatives mentioned above—and this must be carefully argued. In this argument, one cannot simply *presume* either *what* Scripture is, how it is to be read or interpreted, or what "authority" or other relationship to theological reflection it might have. Precisely these questions are the ones to be explored, and they must not be begged in the argument. Until they are settled, and depending on *how* they are settled, we cannot even begin to address the question of the relationship of biblical to systematic theology.

What Reimer calls *systematic* theology, then, has a fundamental priority over what he calls *biblical* theology. Systematic theology must determine *what* the Bible is, and how it is to be used—as well as what *theology* itself is—for the bible itself addresses none of these questions directly. It is not really clear that theology can be based simply or "naturally" on Scripture at all, as Reimer maintains it should be in his basic bi-polar model. In his own way, Reimer acknowledges this priority of theology over Scripture, in his suggestion that both biblical theology and systematic theology are in fact specializations within the wider discipline of Christian theology as a whole. This must mean that their relationship to each other—and each of these itself—is to be understood first of all *theologically*, and only after that, and in the light of that understanding, can biblical material be properly used within theology. But if all of this is true, we need to hear a lot more about how such a basic underlying theological argument addressing these questions is to be carried on, since it is clear that it cannot itself be based directly *on* Scripture. I would like to hear much more about the way in which Reimer would develop these theological questions that arise *prior* to the working out of the relationship between what he has called biblical theology and what he calls systematic theology.

C. *The Problem of Theology's Autonomy and Critical Focus*

We can now see that even to carry out Reimer's own program, theology must be given a certain autonomy over against Scripture, if only to ascertain what Scripture is and how it is to be used. Reimer does give us an important clue to his basic understanding of theology at other places in his paper—where he is not directly addressing the relationship of biblical and systematic theology. For example, in the very first sentence of his paper, he states: "Christian theology . . . is reflection on the grounds, contents, and experience of Christian faith" (p. 37). Later on, he suggests that this reflection leads to an understanding of theology as a kind of trinitarian ontology. By this he means an interpretation of reality and the world, of history and nature, in terms of a particular three-fold structure—"the suprahistorical reality of God, God's self-disclosure *in history* (not *as history*), and God's ongoing presence historically in the life of the church and the world" (p. 47). This interpretation of theology as a kind of trinitarian ontology that focuses every point on *God* is clearly not itself a direct biblical claim; the Bible nowhere directly discusses "ontology." It is a distinctly theological claim, and it provides a way to construe the Bible and certain aspects of many biblical texts, as well as a way to construe reality as a whole. (It is a form of construal with which I am personally in concurrence).

If we make this trinitarian conception our deepest theological insight into reality, and thus the fundamental point of departure for all our theological reflection, and the ultimate criterion of our theological claims and conclusions—as Reimer apparently wishes to do—we will have to take up a rather different stance toward the Bible (and toward biblical theology) than his paper suggests. For in this trinitarian conception it would seem to be *God*, not the Bible, that is to be the ultimate point of reference in terms of which we understand all else. God is the ultimate authority; God is the ultimate source of all reality and truth. So everything is to be understood in relationship to God—this is what the doctrine of the "First Person" is all about.

A central theological question that arises from this point of view is the question, then, of "God's self-disclosure in history," and this is what the doctrine of the "Second Person" deals with: how, when, where does this self-disclosure occur? The answer to these questions will certainly not be: in the Bible—that is, in this particular arbitrary collection of documents. The Bible has never been held to the Second Person of the Trinity. Jesus Christ is the Second Person of the Trinity, but how *that* is to be understood raises many very difficult and disputed theological questions. And the nature of God's "ongoing presence" in history (the "Third Person") similarly opens up important questions that can be answered only by examining what sort of reality history is—how we experience it, what we mean by it, etc.—not simply by looking into the Bible (which does not even have a word for "history"). Doubtless Scripture will have some place in answering many of these theological questions, but many other things will also have a significant place in working out these answers.

It may even turn out, as we work out our answers to these questions about the trinitarian God, that Scripture itself ("what it meant"—Stendahl) will turn out to be seriously misleading in certain respects for our time, in some of the ways that it speaks. One thing that I very much miss in Reimer's conception of theology is a clear acknowledgement that theology has an important *critical* function—in the critique of tradition, and even of biblical ideas and claims. God, as we must conceive God today—if it is truly God in whom we are interested, and not simply *ideas of God* that have been handed down to us from other historical-cultural settings—may now be requiring us to think differently about Godself from the way much tradition and the Bible thought. (The very idea of a trinitarian God is itself a post-biblical idea, as is well known.) To be loyal to God we must be prepared to make such moves: we must not be bound to earlier notions simply because they are traditional (or biblical). One example of this sort of necessary movement in theological thinking has become quite prominent recently: it has to do with the exclusive use of male-gender language and images to conceive of God, a practice that has been oppressive to half the human race, and continues to be oppressive and alienating. Patriarchal linguistic and cultural religious patterns are taken for granted in the Bible, and they are found everywhere in tradition. It is clear that if Scripture is to be used in a theologically valid way—that is, if God is to be treated as God (not simply as the legitimating projection of Israelite patriarchy)—the biblical materials must themselves be criticized theologically, now that we know of the evils of sexism, not simply accepted or followed as we have received them. And this must be done *in the name of God*, the trinitarian God who revealed Godself in history in the past, and continues to reveal Godself in the ongoing history in which we are living.

Jim Reimer seems to allow no place for such a theological critique of biblical claims and the biblical world. Rather, all critique must apparently go in the opposite direction: the biblical world-picture is to stand in criticism of all aspects of our world, never the reverse. This seems to me to be bibliolatry (Bible-idolatry), not theology (thinking about God—the ultimate point of reference that is to order all of our thinking). This position seems to me to involve a fundamental forsaking of Reimer's very proper and profound trinitarian insight, and putting in its place simply the desire to maintain "the old time religion." It is to live in response largely to traditions out of the past, instead of in response to the living activity of the living God today.

I do not wish to pursue these problems further, but this poses my third and last question. Is it finally to be God that we serve in our theological reflection, or is it to be the Bible? These two are not the same, and they cannot be collapsed into each other. If it is to be God, then *theology* will have to be understood rather differently from what Reimer's paper suggests—namely, as concerned essentially with the "explanation, interpretation, and justification" of those "beliefs considered essential and normative for the existence of a particular religious community" (p. 41). And the first reason for undertaking theological reflection surely will have to be something more than merely helping to "inculcate" (p. 50) those beliefs and values in members of the church. Theology will have a much more fundamental purpose than that— namely, to *inspect* those traditional beliefs; to *criticize* them where they have become misleading, dangerously destructive or dehumanizing, in short, idolatrous; and to *reconstruct* them so they can give significant guidance to Christian faith today, as Christians, together with the rest of the human world, face some of the gravest crises of all human history. If one recognizes that it is this very fundamental purpose that motivates and necessitates "reflection on the grounds, contents, and experience of Christian faith" (p. 37), we will be led to a considerably different conception of the relationship between biblical and systematic theology from the one Reimer sketches in his paper.

Chapter 5

Biblical Theology and Feminist Interpretation: A Dinosaur at the Freedom March?

Mary H. Schertz

I
Are Feminists Doing Biblical Theology?

There is something of an enigma surrounding the current relationship between the discipline of biblical theology and the practice of feminist interpretation. While feminist biblical scholars have given very little attention to the theory of biblical theology as a discipline, many of them approach their work from that perspective. A recent issue of *New Testament Abstracts* lists several articles and books written from a clear feminist persuasion under its sections entitled "Biblical Theology."[1] However, none of these entries is theoretical in nature, nor do any of them appear to emerge from a theoretical curiosity about biblical theology as a subject worthy of discussion in itself. They seem, rather, to be directed by an interest in a certain text or biblical theme that summons the writer to a biblical theology approach. In other words, these writers seem to be drawn into doing biblical theology without much self-conscious and reflective thought.

The appearance is that feminist interpreters frequently use the standpoint of biblical theology[2] but do not particularly claim it as their own. If the observation is true, there could be several reasons for it. Perhaps the editors abstracting the articles incorrectly perceive the writers as biblical theologians. Perhaps the mainstream scholars who have struggled to define the discipline of biblical scholars have done it in ways so completely acceptable to feminist scholars that there is no need for them to enter the theoretical discussion.

I doubt, however, that either of these explanations is convincing or sufficiently answers the question of why the topic of the methods and approaches of biblical theology seems to have been met with a resounding silence on the part of feminist exegetes, even as they continue their work as biblical theologians. While the feminist writers may or may not recognize themselves as biblical theologians, these writings fit the category as well as the other articles in the lists of abstracts do. In addition, no feminists "worth their salt" have ever been content to let more traditional scholars set the parameters of their work. Nor can this gap in the scholarship of feminist writers be explained as a disinterest in theoretical matters as such, since the literature in the areas of feminist hermeneutics and interpretation discloses very lively discussions along these lines. Yet any introduction of discussion on "biblical theology" into these conversations about hermeneutics and interpretation has an awkwardness to it. It is almost as if a great, lumbering, gentle, ineffective dinosaur whom everyone had thought to be extinct were to suddenly appear at a political rally. No one seems to be particularly frightened but, although the creature clearly appears to be along for the ride, no one really knows what to do with it, either.

In this essay, I want to look at some of the reasons this conversation between biblical theology and feminist interpretation (as a limited but perhaps representative strand of some of the wider concerns of liberationist thought[3]) seems to be stalemated at worst and awkward at best. First, we will examine some of the different ways of conceptualizing the task of biblical theology in order to determine whether the theoreticians of the discipline have defined it in such a way as to limit its usefulness for feminist perspectives. I will compare and contrast two authors who are post-Bultmannian (in that they posit the same goal for the discipline as Bultmann does while suggesting other categories or methods) with another author who claims a different goal for biblical theology and thus offers something of an alternative to Bultmann. Secondly, I will evaluate these conceptualizations from a feminist perspective. My assumption is that a feminist viewpoint demands certain kinds of "space" from any specific approach. Some of these required "spaces" are room for: taking experience seriously; exposing the biases and prejudices of the interpreter; raising questions of power and authority; and dealing with texts in a dialogical and interactive mode. I will expand on these points by asking the question of what challenges these perspectives offer the discipline of biblical theology. Finally, I plan to explore some components of a potential rapprochement between the disciplines of biblical theology and feminist interpretation. I will argue that if biblical theology is understood to be situated within the more general endeavor of interpretation or hermeneutics and if that location includes a recognition that social analysis is vital to the project, it can be helpful to the enterprise of feminist interpretation of biblical texts.

II
What is Biblical Theology, Anyway?

Let's look first at some contemporary ways of conceptualizing the task of biblical theology. One might ask such questions as: What is the goal of the biblical theology project? Whom or what does it serve? What are the methods being proposed as helpful toward the stated goals and services?

There are at least two different kinds of answers to these questions. One is a post-Bultmannian answer, which is in dialogue with Bultmann and strongly indebted to him. Proponents of these proposals agree with Bultmann that the task of biblical theology is to serve both the sacred texts and contemporary thought by isolating the "kernels" of meaning within the texts and opening them for modern perusal and evaluation. The goal is to derive central statements from the biblical text that can be utilized by the modern world.

The second answer is an answer that may be loosely designated as pragmatic. A proponent of this proposal presents a view that differs from Bultmann's description of the task of biblical theology. In this view, the task of biblical theology is to serve the church. The goal is to help the church engage in critical reflection upon its practice.

The first of these conceptualizations, that of those operating in the tradition of Bultmann, may be represented on the current scene by an article by James M. Robinson on "The Future of New Testament Theology" which appeared in the *Religious Studies Review*, in 1976, and an article by Hendrikus Boers, on "Polarities at the Roots of New Testament Thought," in a collection of essays honoring Frank Stagg, in 1985.[4] Robinson explicitly affirms Bultmann's project. After careful review of the history of the discipline of New Testament theology, he asserts that an expansion of the "front opened up by Bultmann"[5] constitutes one serious positive answer to the question Wrede raised in 1897, about whether there is a future for the discipline. He says that Bultmann not only "went behind" the explicit New Testament doctrines to the understanding of existence objectified in the doctrines, he also traced the "movements" of the New Testament's language to get at the meaning implied. Thus Bultmann exposed an underlying level of understanding of existence that is present in the text latently and implicitly but also actually (p. 20). It is in exposing this layer of meaning that Bultmann successfully fulfills both the historical and normative tasks that, for Robinson, the task of biblical theology comprises.

Exemplary as these efforts are, however, Robinson concedes that Bultmann does need to be "updated." The categories of individualism and existentialism are no longer adequate for our times. Those categories, according to Robinson, need to be expanded—an expansion that needs to take place in a particular direction. It is Robinson's judgment that a move from Bultmann's anthropological categories to ontological categories (considerations of qualities of being) and to cosmological categories (considerations of the social and political issues of the world; p. 21) would facilitate the discovery of the underlying levels of meaning in the text that would enable the contemporary biblical theologian to fulfill likewise the historical and normative tasks required by the discipline.

Thus, for Robinson, the most pressing current task of biblical theology is to make Bultmann's breakthrough "audible" for our age. By contemporizing Bultmann we can help ourselves

move beyond the New Testament doctrinal constructs, which
can only lead us into the business of an antique shop, and
into the movements of language that can be interpreted in
terms of alternatives in the modern world (p. 22).

According to Robinson, biblical theologians ought to move in continuity with
Bultmann's methodology while, at the same time, revising his categories of
meaning in order to present the challenges of the biblical claims in such a way
that they emerge as "a serious alternative for modern times, capable of being
decided for or against, without being falsified in this process of translation
into modern alternatives" (p. 17) Thus, while the method Robinson proposes
remains Bultmann's demythologization, and the goal remains the service of
modern meaning, updating is necessary in the matter of categories. Bultmann's
anthropological approach gives way to an ontological and cosmological
approach.

Hendrikus Boers, on the other hand, while affirming Bultmann's basic program, suggests that new understandings of myth and new methodologies for
working with myth may be needed. Boers takes a position similar to Bultmann
when he says that the "task of interpretation is to move beyond the expressions
to what was expressed."[6] His concern, like that of Bultmann, is to abstract a
"message" to which contemporary Christians can attend without "being dis-
tracted by debates concerning the historicity or mythological nature of the
means of its expression" (p. 60).   Like Robinson, however, he questions
whether Bultmann's existentialist categories of interpretation are adequate for
the contemporary scene. He notes that while existentialist thought was favored
at the time that Bultmann was writing, our own time demands greater attention
to social and historical categories.   Furthermore, he contends, Bultmann's
existentialism has difficulty dealing with fundamental contradictions in a New
Testament concept (p. 60). An example of such a conflict is the long-standing
debate between the notion of salvation as a free gift and salvation as a demand for obedience. What is needed to resolve such a conflict, he says, is a
"better understanding of myth" (p. 61).

This better and more useful understanding of the category of myth can be
found in the methods of structuralism—specifically the structuralism
developed and used by Levi-Strauss and Greimas, because they understand
myth itself as an "attempt to cope with irresolvable contradictions." Such an
approach, Boers feels, allows both poles of the contradiction to retain their
full meaning (p. 61).

To prove his point, Boers proceeds through an exegesis of the conflictual
understandings of salvation and concludes that notions of faith and works are a
fundamental polarity at the root of the New Testament. Some of the New
Testament authors, namely Matthew and John, resolved the polarity in one
direction or the other; others, namely Paul, do not (p. 75). For the purposes of
this essay, the results of Boers's exegesis are not of consequence. Our main

interest is his attempt to contemporize Bultmann by changing the approach and method of working with the phenomenon of myth while essentially retaining and affirming the categories and basic goals of Bultmann's demythologizing project—which provides a vital service to an understanding of contemporary meaning.

In an article entitled "Situating Biblical Theology," which appeared in a 1985 *Festschrift* for Bernhard W. Anderson, *Understanding the Word*,[7] Ben C. Ollenburger proposes an understanding of the goals and methods of the discipline that differs significantly from Bultmann and his disciples. Like Robinson and Boers, Ollenburger develops his argument against the backdrop of the history of the discipline of biblical theology—going back a century earlier than they do to deal with the figure he calls the "'father'" of biblical theology—J.P. Gabler.

Ollenburger makes the point that, historically, the terms of the discipline were set by problems that are no longer problems. In his view, Gabler's arguments for the conjunction of historical assessment (pure biblical theology) and philosophical reflection (true biblical theology) in the practice of biblical theology were postulated largely against Kant's insistence that each of these disciplines "has its own sphere and that the one should not be allowed to legislate the proper activity of the other" (pp. 43, 44). According to Ollenburger, Kant felt that any unification of the discipline of biblical theology (as historical inquiry) and philosophy would be disastrous for each. Theology would need to abandon its reliance upon revelation and subject itself to the rule of reason. In this event, the church would suffer. On the other hand, if philosophy were to be united with the claims of Scripture, it would lose the freedom necessary to its authentic practice (pp. 44, 45).

But, as Ollenburger points out, much has changed in our theoretical and philosophical understandings since the beginnings of biblical theology as a discipline. With the disintegration of the subject-object dichotomy, or what he calls "the collapse of rationalist epistemology" (p. 46), neither the distinction that Gabler makes between historical assessment and philosophical reflection nor the distinction that Kant makes between revelation and reason retain validity. According to Ollenburger,

> History can then be seen as the relation of mind to itself and becomes the object of vigorous philosophical activity; for if history is in some sense the relation of mind to itself, then it is also, in some sense, revelatory of mind. And of course if the mind (or spirit) of which we speaking is Absolute, then history is revelation (p. 47).

Although Ollenburger does not make this connection, it would seem that a perspective denying in this way the validity of the separation of subject and object, assumed by rationalist epistemology, does not only call the earlier distinctions between revelation and reason or pure and true biblical theology into question. Would not the program of demythologization as outlined by Bultmann and affirmed by both Robinson and Boers also be seriously called into question? In my judgment, the program of demythologization is indeed called into question, because it is at heart an effort to de-subjectify an historical text and re-objectify the truth contained within it. If one questions the subject-object dichotomy, then the effort to reject the form of a text while at the same time affirming its content is based upon an insupportable epistemological notion.

Ollenburger continues the argument by addressing the relationship between biblical and systematic theologies—there is a problem with the way this relationship has been conceived. The prevailing assumption (expressed by Gabler but by a whole host of current scholars as well) is that "to be theologically useful in the present, the texts must be removed from the particularities of their own history and culture" (p. 49). In other words, they must be universalized.

There is, Ollenburger suggests, an alternative. First, theology itself has changed and is changing. Beginning with propositional truth or universals is no longer the only way to do theology (p. 49). Secondly, the most important sense in which Scripture functions theologically is in providing an identity for a community. He says:

> Scripture is theologically useful in the first instance, not because it is porous to universally normative explanations, but precisely because in conversation with the historical particularities of its stories and prophecies and proverbs the church is able to sustain its identity as a worshipping, working, protesting community (p. 51).

In short, Ollenburger sees the goal of biblical theology (which he describes as more nearly an activity than a genre) to be "helping the church to engage in critical reflection on its praxis through a self-critical reading of its canonical texts" (p. 51). This goal is accomplished, not by distinguishing sharply between revelation and reason or between true and pure biblical theology, not by demythologizing, not by isolating the essence from the form, not by separating the universal from the particular, not by depending upon a dichotomy between subject and object—but through hermeneutics, through the activity of recovering and discovering the meanings of texts in concrete and critical communities of faith (p. 53). In this context, categories of meaning are developed and used in the interaction between texts and the communities as texts are appropriated. These categories of meaning are, therefore, ultimately dictated by the interactions and connections that communities of faith make between the texts and the contemporary situations in which they find themselves.

Thus we might see Ollenburger's thesis as a live option that should be placed alongside the post-Bultmannian projects as alternate modes of doing biblical theology. We have now defined two basic positions or possibilities.

On the one hand there is the post-Bultmannian option. Proponents of this option are agreed that the goal of biblical theology is to extract universals that can be made available for modern perusal and evaluation. Such persons sometimes disagree on the method—whether it is better to retain the basic project of demythologization or move on to something else such as structuralism.

On the other hand we have a pragmatic option. Proponents of this option contend that the primary goal is to assist the critical reflections of the church while an incidental benefit is to make scripture available to theologies that do not necessarily begin with assumptions about universal truth. The method of this enterprise is hermeneutical and depends upon an understanding that form and content are a unity. The categories are fluid, established in the interaction between the text and the community.

III
What Does Biblical Theology Have to Offer Feminists?

Having sketched two options for doing biblical theology, let us return to the questions with which we began. First, do these theoreticians, as representative of their discipline, define it in such a way as to limit its usefulness for liberation perspectives? Second, do these theoreticians leave the kind of space that is needed for liberationist perspectives to thrive? As noted, these requirements are openness to: the validity of experience as a source of theology; an examination of the biases and prejudices of the interpreter; raising questions of power and authority; a dialogical and interactive mode of dealing with texts. Third, what challenges do these perspectives offer the discipline of biblical theology?

In asking these questions, we need to note that none of these theoreticians directly address the concerns of feminist exegetes or of any other liberation exegete. Neither the post-Bultmannians nor Ollenburger are asking the critical questions from a liberationist perspective. Therefore, any assessments made will necessarily need to be drawn by inference.

While there are some components of Robinson's proposal that feminist exegetes may find useful, he leaves limited space for the kinds of concerns that are foremost in liberationist thought. Robinson's notion that there are levels of meaning that are latent and implicit but actually *there* in the texts is a notion that guides some feminist biblical scholars. Such work has ranged from some of the earlier and more popular efforts to portray the "feminism" of Jesus or Paul to the sophisticated literary analysis of someone like Phyllis Trible, who insists that there is an underlying level of meaning to the Genesis accounts of creation that is affirming of women.[8]

Robinson also makes some room for experiential thinking by opening up the categories of interest to include cosmological concerns. For him, this category of meaning includes social and political issues, issues that are, of course, crucial to feminist as well as other liberationist concerns. In addition to these affinities, Robinson gives something of a bow to a dialogical and critical interaction with the text when he says that the goal of biblical theology is to bring these ancient meanings into modern parlance so that contemporary Christians can choose whether or not to accept them.

But on the whole, though there are some subtle resonances between Robinson's proposal and feminist interpretation, and though one must certainly acknowledge the vast impact Bultmann has had in setting the parameters for any modern discussion of meaning, this proposal does not offer a great deal of help to biblical theologians with liberationist persuasions. While Robinson deals tentatively with the issues of experience and allows that some criticism of the text is in order after the fact, or when the results of the study are complete, he really does not address the issues of power and authority at all.

Boers, on the other hand, offers some substantive insights without going quite far enough in a particular direction to be really helpful to feminist interpreters. He makes some implicit references to the need to expose the biases of the interpreter when he questions the adequacy of Bultmann's existentialist interpretation. He notes that the popularity of existentialism during the period of history in which Bultmann was writing had much to do with Bultmann's existentialist orientation. Likewise, he implies that experience has some influence upon the way we theologize from the texts when he suggests that our present day demands an awareness that places greater emphasis on historical and social modes of thought.

However, Boers's greatest contribution to feminist interpretation may be his insistence that a biblical theology method must be able to cope with the paradoxes and contradictions found within the sacred texts. Feminists have long said that there are conflicting voices and strands of thought within the canon. But Boers's solution leaves little room for the kind of critical reflection that is so vital to feminist interpretation. He suggests that structuralism is a method by which the interpreter can determine whether a biblical author retains a tension or resolves an issue in one direction or another. But he does not suggest that such resolution or lack of it has any ethical impact. He suggests rather that what would be a problem in a group of documents from which one expected some systematic unity is not necessarily a problem in a group of religious writings. In fact, "what appears systematically as a weakness could be a sign of richness" in this "religious framework within which the Christian is called upon to understand herself or himself."[9] This approach is, I suggest, both helpful and somewhat less than helpful. On an issue such as the dichotomy between faith and works, with which Boers is struggling, such an approach can be genuinely helpful. On those issues that can not be morally and ethically compromised, however, such a reconciliation of the different voices within the text raises some profound questions.

Therefore, Boers is both helpful and unhelpful to feminist interpreters. He recognizes the importance of assessing the prejudices of the interpreter, but he does not state why this assessment is so important. He recognizes the contradictions in the texts and offers a way to work with these tensions in a helpful way, but he makes no provision for those tensions that may be ethically irreconcilable from a particular standpoint, such as the feminist point of view. In the end, he leaves some space for liberationist perspectives but not quite enough and not quite the right kind.

To summarize, the post-Bultmannian options resonate with the feminist interpretive project in some ways. There is common ground in the concern for the interplay between text and interpreter, for the biases of the interpreter and for working with paradox and contradiction. There is, however, in these proposals very little room in which to ask the ethical questions, the questions of power and authority that are so important to feminist as well as other liberationist perspectives.

Ollenburger provides more space for the interests of feminist interpreters, largely because in the end he situates biblical theology within the larger rubric of hermeneutics. He notes the "collapse of rationalistic epistemology," and that understandings of theology have changed to accommodate starting points other than abstract universalisms. Then he asserts that the main task of biblical theology is to help the church engage in critical reflection on its praxis through conversation with the particularities of the biblical story. In these understandings and assertions, Ollenburger interjects into the process of biblical theology some of the concerns feminists have for the importance of experience and a dialogical, interactive mode of working with the texts. In addition, as noted, he also accomplishes one of the important moves that must be made in order for feminists to lay claim to the discipline of biblical theology—the location of it within the larger rubric of hermeneutics or interpretation.

As helpful as this proposal is, however, it ends up being like the proposals of Robinson and Boers in that it is two-dimensional rather than three dimensional. In all three of these cases, there is ample discussion of the relationship between the text and its interpreters. True, there are differences in the way the text is perceived among the three, and there is even more difference between the ways the interpreters are perceived. Robinson and Boers imply that the interpreters they have in mind are scholars in search of some kind of meaning, while Ollenburger is explicit that the interpreter he has in mind is the church (or scholars who have the church in mind).[10] But, basically, all three of these proposals deal mainly with the relationship between two dimensions of reality—texts and their readers.

This limited dimensionality is largely due to the failure on the parts of all three theoreticians to address the ethical issues of power and authority[11] in the texts, in our social world, in the academy and in the church. While the biblical texts can and do function in the articulation of contemporary meaning; while they can and do function in the formation of the church's identity; and while they can and do function critically in the church's praxis in the world— the readings of the texts whether by scholars or within the church itself are shaped and controlled by those who hold power and authority. What feminist interpreters and other liberationist interpreters have been saying over and over is that social analysis is a necessary third dimension in the doing of theology. Therefore, while interaction between the texts and scholars can yield statements of meaning, and while interaction between the texts and the communities of faith can help the church reflect critically upon its praxis in the world, neither of these activities is useful for feminists (or for others who care about liberation and justice) unless the interactions are exposed to the clear light of social analysis and ethical judgment. Until awareness of the ethical issues embedded in the act of reading is achieved, there is probably not enough space within the discipline of biblical theology for feminist interpreters to embrace it as a real and ongoing possibility for their work—though I suspect, of course, that many feminist biblical scholars will continue to occasionally practice the discipline.

Thus, I conclude that the while the discipline of biblical theology is not inherently closed to feminist interpreters, the welcome is not an especially warm one either. There is some recognition on the parts of these three theoreticians about the significance of experience, the biases and prejudices of the interpreters and a dialogical, interactive mode of working with texts. While these concerns are not addressed directly, for the most part, there are implications that lead me to believe that biblical theology is, as a discipline, not inherently unsuitable for those interested in incorporating liberationist perspectives into their work with texts. At the same time, the lack of a critical edge, an ethical perspective in these proposals gives pause. That critical edge, of course, has been developed through the route of hermeneutics—via Gadamer, Habermas, Ricoeur, Fiorenza and others. Not surprisingly, the proposal that comes the closest to giving space for ethical discernment in the act of reading and interpreting is the one that situates biblical theology within hermeneutics.

Are we to conclude then that biblical theology is a dinosaur at the freedom rally? Perhaps—at least as the discipline now stands. But before we leave the matter there, let us at least look briefly at another possibility.

I V
A Modest Proposal

I suggest that there is a potential rapprochement between the disciplines of biblical theology and feminist interpretation. I suggest furthermore that there are benefits to such a rapprochement for each discipline.

Such a rapprochement depends upon retaining some aspects of both the post-Bultmannian and the pragmatic approaches to biblical theology. What is important to retain from the pragmatic approach is the conviction that it is necessary to locate the discipline of biblical theology within the larger rubric of hermeneutics. That understanding nurtures the full use of historically particularistic biblical materials (in addition to the more general ones), as Ollenburger is advocating. But that is not all that locating biblical theology within hermeneutics accomplishes.

This understanding of the relationship between biblical theology and hermeneutics also retains a path down which we can walk in the exercise of feminist morality. It is in the tensive connections between messages and their particularisms that we can and must make a very important moral judgment—a judgment that has two steps. The first step has to do with whether the message expands or contracts the historical situation from which it arises. Is the message morally larger or smaller than its context? These being sacred texts, we might approach the question optimistically. Most of the time, the message will morally expand the context. But this optimism is perhaps not universally warranted—some feminists would say that some of the later New Testament texts dilute or distort the gospel message, for instance. The second step has to do with whether the message expands or contracts the contemporary historical contexts to which it speaks—both communal (or ecclesial) and individual (spiritual). Is the message of the text morally larger or smaller than the contemporary contexts? Again, these being our sacred texts, we might approach the question optimistically. Most of the time the message will morally expand these contexts. But, again—perhaps not always, at least if we take the continuing revelation of God seriously.

These judgments necessarily need to be judgments that are carefully considered, but they are legitimately the work of the feminist biblical theologian. The judgments have many linguistic, literary, cultural, historical and theological components—components that will vary according to the type of text being studied. But all such studies have one common element. Social analysis or ethical critical thinking must be a vital part of each judgment, of each operation of these two steps—which brings us back to the aspect of the post-Bultmannians that it is important to retain in a feminist model of biblical theology.

While it is true that biblical theology or its parent rubric, biblical hermeneutics, cannot legitimately abstract messages and throw away their contexts, it is also dangerous and irresponsible to fail to articulate meanings. Biblical stories and metaphors cannot be reduced to propositional statements. There must continue to be direct interaction between communities of faith and the biblical materials in all their particularism. However, from a feminist perspective, our hermeneutics must necessarily take place within an ethical discourse that opposes models of domination and subjugation. This ethical discourse involves an understanding that reading the Bible and describing its meanings are political acts. They are acts that involve the use of power and authority. They are acts that are not equally available to all people. They are acts that have both constructive and destructive possibilities. Until biblical theology recognizes these realities any rapprochement is premature and probably not profitable.

Therefore, it is necessary to protect a critical distance if this ethical dialogue is to take place in healthy and constructive ways. Protecting this distance
may or may not take the shape of demythologization or structuralism. There
would certainly be other options. Sandra Schneiders, for example, speaks of
de-contextualization and re-contextualization in a way that is helpful and
perhaps does not create quite the same problems as the term demythologiztion
on the issue of the subject-object dichotomy.[12] What is important is that a
distance be maintained for critical interaction with the texts. If the methods of
the post-Bultmannians is of somewhat limited use to us as feminist interpreters, their legacy to us is a solid philosophical underpinning for protecting
the kind of space we can use for ethical purposes.

Having put forth these qualifications, I contend that meeting the conditions
is worthwhile for both the enterprise of biblical theology and the enterprise
of feminist interpretation. While it may not be absolutely necessary for
biblical theology to take the issues of *feminist* interpretation seriously, it is
necessary for biblical theology to connect with some contemporary issues in
order to maintain relevancy to the tasks of reading the Bible in the church.
Obviously, not every one in the church agrees with the claims of liberation
theologians. Just as obviously, agree or disagree, the church cannot speak to the
world as it is without understanding and responding to those claims. No less
biblical theology.

A rapprochement is also worthwhile for feminist interpreters. While the
focus of this essay has been the question of whether biblical theology can
accommodate and interest feminist investigation, it is my conviction that
feminist interpreters should extend their practical participation into a concern
about the theoretical definition of the discipline as well. It is not sufficient to
just do biblical theology as feminist interpreters. We must also be concerned
about how it is done. While our hermeneutical work has often led us to new
understandings of the meanings of discrete texts, too often we have not been
able to extend those meanings into a solid understanding of how the Bible
functions in the life of the church. Nor have we been able to derive from our
interpretations of various texts a coherent and consistent challenge for the
church or for individual Christians. Too often, we have left dangling the
questions of what these texts mean for our lives. If we were to take ourselves
more seriously as biblical theologians as well as feminist interpreters, if we
were to contribute to the theoretical definition of the discipline as well as its
practical use, perhaps we could be more useful not only to ourselves but to the
wider church and the wider world. Perhaps we should reconsider the dinosaur.
Perhaps it is not extinct. Perhaps it has a place in the freedom march after all.
Perhaps it belongs to us also.

Notes

1   A recent issue of *New Testament Abstracts*, for instance, listed the following titles under its "Biblical Theology" section: *Mary, Woman of Nazareth: Biblical and Theological Perspectives; The Case for Women's Ministry: Biblical Foundations in Theology*; and *White Women's Christ and Black Women's Jesus: Feminist Christology and Womanist Response* (NTA 34 [1990]: 262, 263).

2   There is no single, identifiable standpoint for the discipline of biblical theology, of course.   The phenomenon that I am noting here has a counterpart on the wider scene.   The academy lacks consensus as to what the discipline is all about, but plenty of people are just going ahead and doing it.

3   In this essay, I regard feminist perspectives to be a subcategory of liberationist perspectives.   While I will sometimes appear to be using the categories interchangeably, I mean to denote those areas and ways the two perspectives intersect and overlap—I do not mean to collapse one into the other.

4   Robinson, "The Future of New Testament Theology," *RSR* 2 (1976): 17-23; Boers, "Polarities at the Roots of New Testament Thought," in *Perspectives on the New Testament*, ed. C. H. Talbert (Macon, GA: Mercer University Press, 1985), 55-75.

5   Robinson, "New Testament Theology," 20.   Page numbers immediately following in the text refer to Robinson's article.

6   Boers, "Polarities," 60.   Page numbers following in the next refer to Boers's article.

7   JSOTSS, 37 (Sheffield: JSOT Press, 1985), 37-62.   Page numbers following in the text refer to Ollenburger's article.

8   See her *God and the Rhetoric of Sexuality* (Philadelphia: Fortress Press, 1978), and the companion volume, *Texts of Terror* (Philadelphia: Fortress Press, 1984).

9   Boers, "Polarities," 29.

10   Both Robinson and Ollenburger talk about a third party but, in my opinion, these third parties do not constitute other dimensions that exert any real "pull" in the process of biblical theologizing.   For Robinson, this third party consists of the people (presumably the Christians) who will decide for or against the meanings proposed by the scholars when the research is done. These are the people for whom the studies are done, but they do not play an integral role in the process of the studies themselves.   For Ollenburger, this third party consists of the systematic theologians who may incidentally reap the benefits of the biblical theologians' work.   These are not the people for whom the studies are done, and they play no role in the research, but they may accidentally benefit from the work of the biblical theologians.

11   While Ollenburger uses the word 'authority' frequently, on pp. 49-50 ("Biblical Theology"), he is defending particularistic texts as equally authoritative with more general texts.

12   Sandra M. Schneiders, "Feminist Ideology Criticism and Biblical Hermeneutics," *BTB* 19 (1989): 3-10.

Chapter 6

Theology in Transition
Toward a Confessional Paradigm for Theology

Howard John Loewen

I
Theology and Paradigm Shifts

A. *Theology in Crisis*

Thesis: The presenting problem of the relationship of biblical and systematic theology is derivative of the larger issue of the relationship between biblical exegesis and theological reflection in a confessional community. Ultimately, it is derivative of the nature and function of theology itself.

In his most recent work, *Theology for the Third Millennium*, Hans Küng contends that the church and theology are in a crisis period of transition between the modern period and an emerging post-modern period. The notion that western culture is experiencing the throes of a major paradigm shift is not new, of course. Such observations have been coming from various fields of study for some time. What is distinctive about Küng's proposal is his application of the concept of paradigm change to the entire history of the church and theology. He contends that there have been a number of major shifts in the "total constellation of convictions, values, and patterns of behavior" in the history of the church and in western society as a whole. He argues that we are currently in the midst of another "epochal threshold," from modernity to postmodernity.[1]

Küng maintains that only when theology has resolved the classical conflicts that remained unresolved from previous epochal shifts will it be prepared to work out future perspectives and be adequately prepared for the third millennium.[2] For him, the heart of those classical conflicts revolves around issues of how we understand Scripture in relation to tradition and theology. Put more precisely, "What role do we assign to the discipline of expounding Scripture—exegesis—in relation to the discipline that systematically ponders the content of faith—dogmatics."[3] Küng is convinced that there cannot be a truly evangelical and ecumenical theology until there is some consensus on this issue.

Küng's identification of the problem in this manner is important for our discussion here, for the presenting problem in this collection of essays has been articulated in terms of the relationship between biblical and systematic theology. Yet the issue at hand is certainly deeper than the nature of the relationship between two disciplines in theology. It is my contention that we are dealing here with the nature of the theological task itself, related to our understanding of Scripture as canon.

The purpose of this paper will be to take seriously Küng's call to address the contemporary crisis in theology from a historical perspective. For it is clear that "one cannot do justice to the present crisis in theological orientation if it is isolated. If something helpful is to be said to the crisis, one must be aware that the difficulties indicated did not originate from modern times."[4]

My approach will be to present the basic models which are representative of the way in which the Christian tradition has conceptualized the nature and task of theology in relationship to its use of Scripture. I will also attempt to provide an understanding of the social location which gave rise to the various approaches.

A central thesis in this study is that the presenting problem of the relationship of biblical and systematic theology is a derivative of the larger issue of the relationship between biblical exegesis and theological reflection in the church. Or, put another way, the critical issue is the theological use of Scripture in the hermeneutical context of confessional Christian communities. In conjunction with this way of putting the question we will also discuss one of the major ways in which the Bible has been appropriated in theological reflection in the contemporary period.

The construal of the relationship between biblical exegesis and theological reflection is inextricably linked to one's understanding of the nature and role of 'theology.'[5] Therefore, we will also attempt to propose an historically sensitive and hermeneutically sound conception of theology in light of the classical models and within the framework of the contemporary hermeneutical discussion.

II
Development of the Classical Models in Theology

B. *Theology as Knowledge*

Thesis: In the early church period biblical exposition and theological reflection in the context of the church were inseparable. Theology was centered on the interpretation of Scripture. There was no distinction between biblical exegesis and the theological interpretation of Scripture and thus no understanding of having different disciplines in theology.

The first model of theology emerges in the first several centuries of the early church period as the Christian faith makes its transition from first-century Jewish Christianity, with its apocalyptic paradigm, to the early Catholicism with its more Hellenistic paradigm.

According to Rogers, early on the teachers of the church wrestled with the problem of their twofold environment, the Jewish and the Greek, and some coopted philosophy in the service of their cause, wrestling with the relationship of the Bible, faith, and reason. Yet in the main, the Bible was a resource of primary data, accepted by faith, from which reasoned conclusions could be drawn. The Apologists "exegeted typologically in the context of the kerygma, the central gospel message, the pattern of Christian truth recognized by the church." [6]

Farley concurs that from early on the church wrestled with the relationship of the Bible and reason. But the polemical and systematic expositions were not seen as part of a 'science' in the later Aristotelian sense of a demonstrative undertaking. Rather, the task of theology was understood in terms of appropriating the knowledge of God as revealed in Scripture. [7]

According to Farley, understanding theology as salvific knowledge of God as revealed in Scripture was very much a part of the Christian movement and its literature. In fact, a salvifically oriented knowledge of divine being was part of the Christian community and tradition long before it was named 'theology.' [8] As Rogers argues, the accessibility of this kind of knowledge presupposed a strong affirmation of the incarnational concept of God accommodating to the human situation. It enabled theologians to take seriously both the human textual matrix and the divine theological meaning. It functioned to modify the prevailing philosophical forms of thought adopted from the Greek environment. The theological emphasis was not philosophical but a salvifically oriented knowledge of God. [9] This emphasis on God's incarnational and redemptive relationship to the world ultimately finds significant expression in the ecumenical creeds which reflect the outcome of the early theological controversies.

Thus, according to Pannenberg what we today call theology was in the early church centered on the interpretation of Scripture. During this period the expositional and systematic functions of theology were not separate. Only at the end of the second century was there typological interpretation of the Old Testament with reference to Christ, followed by interpretation of the New Testament writings and commentaries on them. The critical issue here is the employment of the allegorical method to demonstrate the unity of Old and New Testaments. But there was no distinction between the historical and systematic interpretation of Scripture, and thus no understanding that there were different disciplines in theology. [10]

For Farley, "the great teachers of the church . . . engaged in what now could be called inquiry, a discipline of thought and interpretation occurring in their commentaries on Scripture and in their polemical and pedagogical writings." He states that their effort had primarily the character of exposition, the interpretation of the received text from Scripture or council (Farley, 33).

But significant differences began to develop regarding the use of Scripture in theological formulations. There was, on the one hand, a major representative like Origen, whom Rogers calls a "'man of the Book' who studied the Bible more thoroughly than any theologian of his time. He was at the same time a 'man of his age.' He imbibed the reigning philosophy and did his best to make Christianity credible in Platonic categories." He "moved beyond the common typological interpretations of previous church teachers to solve difficult problems through allegorical exegesis," and also "produced the first systematic theology of the Christian era," sometimes changing the meaning of the biblical message to fit the system (Rogers and McKim, 15).

Church theologians like Origen, and Clement before him, represented the more western Alexandrian school, where the biblical truth was increasingly given distinctive shape by systematic and philosophical reason. On the other hand was the Antiochean school of theology and exegesis. It represented more the eastern Mediterranean world. According to Rogers, it had a "stronger feeling for the human element in the biblical writings and for the historical reality of biblical revelation" (Rogers and McKim, 16). It represented a grammatical-historical method of biblical interpretation. As Rogers points out, its most noted teacher was Chrysostom. Yet he shared in common with the Alexandrian school "the early church's view that God had accommodated his teaching to our capacities for understanding," most notably in the incarnation of Jesus Christ. He urged people to read the Bible. He shared with the chief theologians of the early church the full acceptance of "the authority of Scripture and attributed its saving message to God" (Rogers and McKim, 20). For Chrysostom, "theology was a practical not a theoretical calling. The biblical message made a difference in people's lives" (Rogers and McKim, 21).

Thus, in this earliest paradigm of Christian thought, theology had the basic character of being divine, sapiential knowledge, revealed in Scripture for the practical purpose of bringing salvation to the lives of people through the church (Farley, 29-33). Its significance was profoundly linked to God's redemptive nature and to the spiritual disposition of God's people. This model needs to be distinguished from what developed later in the medieval period. But before we move to that discussion, I need to say something about the transitional period between the two. The developments here can best be represented by Augustine who, by most estimates, was a transitional figure between the early and medieval periods, and whose own understanding of biblical interpretation and theological reflection profoundly shaped the direction in which theology moved.

Rogers points out that, like most of the church theologians before him, Augustine had a strong view of God's incarnation and accommodation to history as revealed in Jesus Christ. He instinctively understood that faith was needed to seek understanding and that the primary purpose of Scripture was to bring us into a practical and personal knowledge of faith (Rogers and McKim, 27). Augustine's method of interpretation was, in the main, concerned with the "practical fruits of Scripture study" (Rogers and McKim, 32). Yet the new emphasis in Augustine was the need for the church's authority in interpreting Scripture. Rogers aptly describes those developments:

> An outgrowth of the interaction of church and Scripture was the *regula fidei, the rule of faith. There was in circulation in the church a brief creedal formula. It was probably originally a baptismal formula that had been elaborated for use in instructing new members of the church. Around this core statement of faith were grouped a series of fundamental doctrines of the Christian faith acknowledged as essential by the church. This creedal statement and these doctrines were traditionally attributed to Christ himself, as communicated through the apostles. . . . Through this appeal to the regula fidei as an interpreting principle, Augustine was kept in touch with the kerygma, the central saving message of the church (Rogers and McKim, 34).

This development, as represented in Augustine, is most significant in that the established norms for theology as knowledge, in the classical period of Christianity, were these articles of faith themselves. As Farley states, "These doctrines of church tradition were not products, accomplishments of theology, but the 'principia,' the givens. They were the norms for interpreting Scripture and determining Christian truth and responsibility." (Farley, 41).[11] This generally characterized the theological task in the premodern period. As we shall see, the solidification of this emphasis also had significant implications for the relationship of Scripture to theology in the medieval period.

C. Theology as Science

1. The Emergence of the Medieval Model. Thesis: In the medieval period there was a gradual separation of the exegetical task from theological reflection within the context of the establishment of Christendom, the revival of Aristotelian studies, and the development of Scholasticism.

In this second paradigm, we have moved from the world of the early church in a Hellenistic context to the world of the medieval, Roman Catholic church, where the final shape of theology finds its culmination in Thomas Aquinas. Politically, the Middle Ages marked the end of the Roman Empire and the coming into being of Europe as a political entity; ecclesiastically, [it] "was that period when the Roman church claimed to be the one true state." Intellectually, "both of the major ancient philosophical schools, that of Plato and that of Aristotle," were carried on into this period (Rogers and McKim, 35).

During the early Middle Ages, theologians continued the Augustinian attitude toward the authority and interpretation of the Bible (Rogers and

McKim, 37). However, a different approach began to emerge in theological studies. Beyond the reading of the texts, from Scripture and the church theologians, and the lectures on them, there was introduced the argument, at first to clear away linguistic and grammatical difficulties and later to harmonize authorities" (Rogers and McKim, 38). This method reflects the medieval juridical pattern.

The study and interpretation of texts later took on a standardized four-step form: question, provisional answer, objection, and definitive answer. Accordingly "the methodology shifted the focus...from faith in the authority to the reasons why an opinion was held" (Rogers and McKim, 38). There were those theologians whose "aim was to provide a complete, rational explanation of Christian doctrine as found in the Bible and the church fathers" (Rogers and McKim, 38). The authority of Scripture and creeds was not questioned, but reason and authority tended to be seen as coming from one source of divine wisdom, and they could not contradict each other.

Thus there came about a philosophical shift that finally led to Platonic thought being replaced by Aristotelian reasoning and the appeal to an open mind (Rogers and McKim, 39-40). Soon there would be developments that would lead to giving reason priority over the Bible. Stronger claims would be made for human reason outside the realm of faith commitment, as for example in Anselm. Gradually, reason came to have a more unquestioned superiority.

According to Rogers, the logic of Aristotelian Scholasticism

> shaped the style of academic teaching by placing a premium on accuracy of form and subtlety of expression, rather than on practical consequences in life. The thirteenth century saw a revival of Aristotelian studies. Logic replaced discovery (Rogers and McKim, 36).

Thus, Rogers continues,

> scholasticism represented a movement away from the early church's common foundations of theological method and its approach to the Bible. . . . The developments were uneven, but the direction is discernible. Christian doctrine was organized, sorted out, and classified as a body of knowledge to be analyzed and expounded by human reason (Rogers and McKim, 37).

Abelard symbolized this shift in emphasis. Again as Rogers points out, his book, *Theologia Christiana*, introduced the term 'theology' in the sense it had subsequently—a body of doctrine that could be analyzed. He organized all doctrines under the headings of faith, love, and sacrament. The church fathers had never used 'theology' in that sense to refer to Christian doctrine (Rogers and McKim, 41-42).

Peter Lombard advanced this emphasis in his work, *Four Books on Sentences*, which represents a collection of the annotations and commentaries on texts of

Scripture and the church theologians. Rogers states that "the texts and commentaries were organized into four books on the plan of the chronological order of the history of salvation: God, creation, redemption, and the sacraments and eschatology." This book became the standard theological textbook until the Reformation, and "its style and plan of organization influenced the subsequent *Summas* by Thomas Aquinas and others" (Rogers and McKim, 42).

According to Rogers,

> these theological texts were studied and expounded far more than the Scriptures during the Scholastic era. They focused the attention of theologians on traditions and the opinions of theological schools. Aristotelian logic, as a means of resolving contradictions among traditional opinions, was . . . the operative norm by which theological decisions were made (Rogers and McKim, 42).

Pannenberg summarizes the developments of the medieval period well. According to him, there appeared alongside scriptural commentaries, not only didactic and occasional writings of various sorts, but also collections of sayings of the Fathers. They attempted to resolve the contradictions in the Fathers, but now lost their connection with the exposition of Scripture and were collected by topic and compared for compatibility by the dialectical method, an approach which developed and increased (Pannenberg, 352).

Pannenberg states that the biblical texts tended to become obscured in the teaching of theology by the proliferation of *quaestiones*. Accordingly, this is the point at which systematic theology's growth into an autonomous discipline began—a shift of interest towards the systematic relevance of the material contained in scripture and the patristic tradition, as a result of the *sententia*. According to Pannenberg, many see this as a normal development of theology into an organized science. Hence theology as a science was born (Pannenberg, 352-53). This, according to Farley, created a new distance among Bible, theology, and the church (Farley, 38).

In this regard, Pannenberg states that in the Middle Ages, as was to be the case in scholastic Protestantism, exegesis was enclosed within the frontiers fixed by systematic theology. Aristotelian scholasticism greatly shaped Christian theology in Catholicism and Protestantism alike. Hence, theology in the strict sense was the total explication of Christian doctrine, proceeding by systematic methods and normative for exegesis. This, Pannenberg says, explains why there was no incentive for systematic theology to seek independence from scriptural interpretation, for it had successfully circumscribed it and brought it into its own orb (Pannenberg, 353). As Rogers states, "textbook Thomism in the seventeenth century put reason prior to faith, emphasized proofs for the existence of God, and accented the words of the Bible interpreted according to a logical system rather than the meaning of Scripture interpreted in its historical context" (Rogers and McKim, 47)

There was, then, a major transition of Christian learning and teaching based on Scripture into an Aristotelian science located in centers of learning. Theology became a faculty in the university, a deliberate and methodological undertaking whose end was knowledge (Rogers and McKim, 43-44). Farley maintains, somewhat more optimistically, that in this period theology was still wisdom, but wisdom deepened and extended significantly by human study and argument. He states that what gave this period its unity was the coming together of the classical patristic doctrinal scheme and the school (Farley, 51-52).

According to Farley, the result was the appropriation of learning, especially from philosophy, into a framework to explore and express the classical scheme. It resulted in *theologia* as *scientia*, in the distinctive scholastic sense of a method of demonstrating conclusions. The distinction between theology as knowledge and theology as discipline was sharpened, a trend that ultimately led to its division. One strand of late scholastic thought developed the science, the other the mystical knowledge. The former development dominated the latter. The separation was finalized in the modern period (Farley, 51-52).

2. The Rejection of the Scholastic Model. Thesis: The Reformation represents a rejection of the Aristotelian-Scholastic method of understanding and interpreting the Bible, and a reaching back to the understanding of Scripture and theology in the early church period.

The medieval paradigm, characterized by the synthesis of faith and reason in theology, began to disintegrate in the late thirteenth and fourteenth centuries, through the work of such theologians as Scotus and Occam, and also through such pre-Reformers as Wycliffe and Hus. The separation of the spheres of theology and science in the pre-Reformation period, with their own criteria of validation, opened up the possibility of viewing theology once again as a more practical discipline and reasserting the primacy of the Bible's authority in fulfilling the theological task (Rogers and McKim, 45-46, 74-75). The basis for this development was the nominalist claim that theology could not be a science because its assertions were based on faith not reason (Rogers and McKim, 80).

The Reformation itself, therefore, represents a rejection of an Aristotelian-Scholastic method of understanding and interpreting the Bible. Luther reached back to the attitudes of the early church by regarding the Bible's purpose as salvation and guidance in the life of faith. Calvin influenced by his humanist training focused on the plain and practical meaning of the biblical text. Thus, both Luther and Calvin were primarily 'biblical' theologians, as their many commentaries witness. They saw the task of theology to be both pastoral and pedagogical (Rogers and McKim, 92).

The Radical Protestant wing of the Reformation, together with Luther and Calvin, also reasserted the principle of *sola scriptura*. They particularly emphasized the concrete practice of biblical faith. They brought into central focus themes such as costly discipleship, the visible church and its mission, adult baptism, and the way of love and nonresistance to express their radical biblicist perspective.

The various attacks of the Protestant Reformation on scholastic theology were significantly based on biblical interpretation—and on the hermeneutical assumption that the Bible is its own interpreter—even though this did not lead to the establishment of biblical theology as an autonomous discipline, as we have since come to know it. The only immediate effect was to keep the systematic treatment of Christian doctrine closer to the content of the biblical texts than it had been during the Scholastic period. The reformers accepted the ancient creeds, not so much because the councils of the church had ratified them, but because their content conformed to Scripture (Rogers and McKim, 77). Even the Anabaptists generally assumed the validity of the creeds, although, within the sixteenth century context, they did not appeal to their authority in any explicit sense.

Thus, the Reformation itself represents a paradigmatic shift away from the model of theology as a science. It moved toward reappropriating the model of the earlier church period. However, within the course of several generations, there was a return to the medieval paradigm of theology as a science, even though it was now manifested also in a Post-Reformation Protestant Scholasticism, in addition to the newly reasserted Counter-Reformation, Catholic Scholasticism. Scholasticism did not cease to exist, despite the strong Protestant reaction to it. In fact, it seems to have returned with greater strength.

3. The Reassertion of the Scholastic Model. Thesis: In the Post-Reformation period there was a gradual transition from the more Augustinian orientation to Scripture and theology, fostered by the mainline Reformers, to a full-blown Protestant Scholasticism, which now took its position beside the newly reasserted Catholic Scholasticism of the Counter-Reformation.

Whereas the Reformers "had taught theology primarily through exegesis of biblical passages" the new scholasticism once again "felt obliged to clarify and systematize the passages cited" (Rogers and McKim, 162). Increasingly, Scripture and doctrine became separated, and theology, even more than before, was viewed "as a scholastic science instead of a practical discipline" (Rogers and McKim, 163).

In this environment of a renewed Aristotelian scholasticism,

> theology was no longer viewed as a practical, moral discipline exclusively directed toward the salvation of people and their guidance in the life of faith. Instead, it now became an abstract, speculative, technical science that attempted to lay foundations for philosophical mastery of all areas of thought and life (Rogers and McKim, 148).

God now supplied scientific information, and "the Bible became a book of delivered truths" (Rogers and McKim, 166). The new science and philosophy rejected all appeals to authority, and increasingly placed its confidence in human reason, intuition, or experience where God's truth was inferred from nature or humanity.

The post-Reformation scholastic theologies "placed great emphasis on precise definition and systematic, scientific statement" (Rogers and McKim, 173). Theology and Scripture became the formal principles of dogmatics on which to construct the material doctrinal issues into a scientific theology. Scripture took on the formal role of an epistemological principle rather than a soteriological function.

Rogers states that "scholasticism structured theology as a logical system of belief in reliance on Aristotelian syllogistic reasoning. The emphasis was on a rational defense of a settled deposit of doctrines" (Rogers and McKim, 187-88). Protestant scholasticism

> substituted philosophical speculation for growth in the Christian life as the goal of theological work. Once again theology attempted to return to the medieval ideal of being the queen of the sciences. A total unified system of knowledge was desired rather than just a deepened insight into Christian faith (Rogers and McKim, 186).

What do we make, then, of the relationship between biblical interpretation and the developments in systematic theology in this period? Two things should be noted. First, in Catholic theology, alongside the scholastic theological developments there was the development of a 'positive' (i.e,. exegetical) theology already in the sixteenth century. Second, in Protestant theology, as we have already indicated, there was the rehabilitation of, or unfortunate return to, a scholastic and academic theology alongside scriptural interpretation, after the beginning of the seventeenth century. According to Pannenberg, it was these developments that finally brought biblical-exegetical and systematic theology to co-exist as disciplines for the first time in the post-Reformation period. Thus, notes Pannenberg, by 1628 the term 'exegetical theology' (earlier called 'positive theology') appeared in George Calixt's *Apparatus theologicus* (Pannenberg, 354).

D. Theology as Practice

Thesis: With the emergence of the modern enlightenment period the distinction between exegetical and systematic theology was increasingly solidified, thereby separating the historical and dogmatic elements in theology.

As we have intimated, the separation between exegetical and systematic theology came about as a result of the development of the concept of a biblical theology as distinct from scholastic or dogmatic theology. Simultaneously, systematic theology, since the beginning of the seventeenth century, was also establishing its own legitimate place. Pannenberg points out that the proposal for a biblical dogmatics as distinct from the scholastic form was now soon superseded by the distinction between biblical studies (which increasingly saw its work as history) and dogmatics of any sort. Biblical theology thus came to be understood as a historical discipline (Pannenberg, 356).

Therefore, the separation of the systematic and historical elements in theology (and thus systematics from history, and biblical theology from dogmatics) to form distinct disciplines is a relatively recent event in the history of the church. Similarly, other theological disciplines have also acquired autonomy at various times since the Renaissance/Reformation period.

Farley says that the distinction between Scripture interpretation and dogmatics happened quite naturally under the circumstances subsequent to the post-Reformation period. For them to be firmly established as distinct sciences, the critical principle and historical method of the Enlightenment had to be applied to the study of Scripture. Then exegetical theology, as a historical discipline, could become a separate scholarly discipline with its own methods, and dogmatics could be distinguished from it by a larger complex of materials (creeds, confessions, doctrines) and a different method. Eventually a fourfold encyclopedic division developed out of this fundamental distinction between the exegetical/historical and dogmatic/practical: Bible, church history, dogmatics, and practical theology, a pattern which, according to Farley, ultimately departs from the material unity of theology (Farley, 39-44, 50-54, 77-80, 89-90).

Yet it should be noted that exegetical/biblical theology in the pre-encyclopedia period would not be thought of as a discrete science, but rather as the study of the writings where God's revealed Word was found (Farley, 51, 54-55). However, as Farley points out, by the late nineteenth and in the twentieth centuries, specialists in the biblical area tended not to think of their subject matter that way—as revelation occurring in and with the texts of their specialty. More typical was the attempt to define the discipline or science, not by the collection, but by the historical phenomenon—the religion of Israel or the origins of Christianity (Farley, 107).

In regard to systematic theology, Pannenberg notes that the concept of systematic theology came into theology in the seventeenth century, after the introduction of the concept of 'system' into theology to describe the theology known as scholastic academic theology (Pannenberg, 404) The first use of the term *theologia dogmatica* was in 1659. Dogmatics provided a unified discussion and summary of the content of Scripture. Later it came to be known as systematic theology (Pannenberg, 405-06).

In the eighteenth century the term systematic theology included only dogmatics and moral theology. Later came its development into independent disciplines, and the transition from polemics to symbolics to denominational studies to modern ecumenical studies. Apologetics as a separate discipline only emerged at end of eighteenth century. However, the designation 'systematic theology' became more and more inadequate, since the investigation of the nature and truth of Christianity became a specialized area, and not a shared responsibility of Christian theology as a whole (Pannenberg, 410-11).

Farley, even more than Pannenberg, decries the direction in which theology has gone in the modern period. He contends that, subsequent to the post-Reformation era, theology continued to undergo such radical transformation that the original senses of theology as salvific, sapiential knowledge, and as a full-fledged scientific discipline, virtually disappeared; effectively, effectively another paradigm emerged. Theology as a personal quality continued, not under the term theology, not as a salvation-disposed wisdom, but as the practical know-how necessary to ministerial functions in the church. For Farley, this is an outcome of theology's long career as an Aristotelian science (Farley, 109-16).

According to Farley, this paradigmatic shift to theology as practice was inaugurated by two movements: continental Pietism and the Enlightenment. Both constituted a basic critique of the scholastic theologies. These movements had the effect of precipitating a fundamentally different approach to theology (Farley, 56-65).

Farley gives considerable attention to the significant influence Schleiermacher had on this shift by articulating a formal framework for it. For Schleiermacher, theology is not a science in the pure sense but in the sense of "a theory for an area of social practice." What unifies theology for him is "the social situation of clerical praxis external to the university and the faculty of theology." Hence, theology is the knowledge needed by the clerical leadership in the social ordering of specific religious communities (Farley, 87). He thus replaces traditional doctrinal truths with a focus on practice and experience as the subject matter. Theology is no longer knowledge in the classical sense, but clearly an objective referent of knowledge whose categories are set by what is needed for the social ordering of the church.

In Schleiermacher's scheme, those categories became practical theology, historical theology, and philosophical theology. The material unity of this scheme replaced the theological unity of the earlier scheme of Scripture, church history, and dogmatics. By adding the area of practical theology to the earlier threefold scheme, Schleiermacher secured the fourfold scheme of the theological encyclopedia. For Schleiermacher, the unity of theology as a positive science lies in its capacity to educate the leadership of a living community. According to Farley, this represents a shift from a scientific to a ministerial paradigm, with primarily a functional, rather than theological, unity (Farley, 85-86, 88-89).

In this way, according to Farley, theology became a study of discrete disciplines pertinent to ministry. Theology as a discipline involving a single science was lost. The literary expression of this plurality was the theological encyclopedia. Here theology becomes one of the specialties along with biblical studies, ethics, pastoral care, etc., largely in the form of systematic theology. Each of these specialties must somehow be made personally relevant for faith and life. Theology thus attends to the course and conduct of Christian life. It is now the means toward the end, the holy life. This, in Farley's view, is a serious form of reductionism, for it objectifies theology. Theology is a sort of objectified teaching to be translated toward the practical end of training clergy (Farley, 8-94, 110-11).

In this paradigm, theology is no longer defined by its ability to communicate salvific knowledge or to name divine truths. Rather, it is thought of as a collection of truths from which a bridge must be built toward practical ends. Thus, according to Farley, theology has shifted from being (a) salvific, sapiential knowledge, to (b) doctrinal truths themselves in a unified science, to (c) practical training for ministry (Farley, 127-35). He correctly notes that buried in this paradigm shift of the modern period is the issue of the meaning of theology itself, for there has been a major shift from a theocentric to an anthropocentric focus, from God's own self-knowledge to emphasis on present practice of the Christian life. We will return to this point. However, before we do, we must consider a major transitional development in the contemporary period of the church.

III
Development of a Contemporary Model in Theology

E. Theology as Hermeneutics
Thesis: With the complete separation between the interpretation of the biblical text and its theological use in the context of the interpreter during the last several centuries, the late modern period has seen the emergence of another theological paradigm—theology as hermeneutics. This development has corresponded with the contemporary shift in the toward the cultural and contextual.

1. *The Development of Theology as Hermeneutics.* The modern period represents a turn toward the historical, the anthropological, and the sociological dimensions of reality. It involves a shift from source to situation. This shift has been accompanied by a relativization of the traditional theological sources of authority—Scripture, theological tradition, and the teaching ministry of the church—and thus of the content of theology itself. The shift from content to context has greatly affected our understanding of the theological task. It has particularly brought into focus the question of how world views are constructed, and how one brings together the world of the contemporary interpreter and the world of the text. How do we move from our horizon toward a fusion of our world with that of the world of the text?[12] These developments have given birth to another paradigm for understanding Scripture and the task of theology—theology as hermeneutics.[13]

According to Wood, the world of the text and the role and context of the interpreter were increasingly separated. Interpreting the text has become a descriptive historical function, in which the interpreter's disposition to the text is not a factor in understanding it. Yet today that viewpoint is seriously questioned.[14] Accordingly, "one of the most intriguing developments in recent general hermeneutics is the acknowledgement that the question of one's understanding of a text cannot be intelligibly discussed apart from the question of the use one has made or is prepared to make of it." Wood says that "an explicit acknowledgment of the relationship between understanding and use can have some important consequences for the discipline of interpretation known as theological hermeneutics."[15]

In this emerging paradigm the task of theology is not simply a question of determining the meaning of biblical texts, but of ascertaining the Christian understanding and appropriation of those texts. That determination is part of the larger and total task of theological reflection and cannot be relegated to one or another discipline, such as biblical or systematic theology, or to some inadequate relationship between the two. It is a more basic and primary theological task that the church must once again reinstate and appropriate. The fundamental issue is not the relationship of biblical and systematic theology, but the very nature, meaning, and role of theology itself.

It is, therefore, a significant step forward explicitly to conceptualize the task of theology once again as hermeneutical, for theology is fundamentally interpretational in nature.[16] In my judgment, it is not adequate, in the late modern and emerging postmodern period, to formulate the task of theology simply as knowledge, or as science, or as practice. In a very real sense, these emphases must all be included in a full-orbed understanding of the hermeneutical nature of theology. But we will return to that point later. Here it will be helpful to illustrate the hermeneutical nature of theology from the thought of David Tracy.

For Tracy, the main task of theology is "the ever new interpretation of the text of Christian tradition for the respective situation." It is, he says,

> concerned with the specifically Christian confession of faith
> in the God of Jesus Christ, a profession which has become
> expressed in the texts, symbols, formulae and prayers of
> the Christian tradition. This activity is hermeneutical
> throughout. The interpretation of the Christian texts con-
> tributes to a disclosure of the truth present in the texts.[17]

On this reading, exegesis is also theological, and interpretation is the business of theology. Thus, for Tracy, theology as hermeneutics affirms the conversational nature of the interpretive task, acknowledging the autonomy of the text and the historical intersubjective framework of every interpreter within a community of readers. It takes its orientation from the reader, but it allows justice to be done to the text. The text and the reader (in community) stand in a dialectical relationship to each other.[18]

In this view of Scriptural understanding and theological reflection, the basic question is not the relationship of biblical and systematic theology. Nor is the most basic question how one relates biblical exegesis and theological interpretation. But the question is, rather this: how does one's hermeneutical understanding of the biblical text relate to one's hermeneutical understanding of the contemporary situation. One must read hermeneutically both the Scriptures and the situation today in order to fulfill and complete the task of theological interpretation. According to Tracy, the aim of all hermeneutical endeavors in Christian theology is transformative in nature. Therefore, our interpretational situation is, in each case, just as much the object of theological interpretation as are the biblical texts themselves, through which our situation is brought into fuller view. Therefore, theology as hermeneutics involves a double interpretational venture.[19]

Tracy contends that, in the hermeneutical paradigm, the Bible is seen as itself grounded in hermeneutical experience. We are only able to acknowledge the transforming power of the biblical text when we read (i.e, interpret) it. The Bible must be understood in terms of the reception of its normative message and norming power to defend itself against any definitive interpretation, and to disclose transformative truth.[20] Thus, for Tracy, theology is open to unplanned interpretational results, to unsuspected changes of the interpretative perspective, and of the situation of interpretation itself.[21]

2. A Hermeneutical Understanding of Bible and Theology. But we must return to the question of the relationship of biblical and systematic theology, and again evaluate its status within the framework of this paradigm. With respect to so-called systematic theology, I would agree that assigning primarily to systematic theology, as one of the modern theological disciplines, the task of developing concrete interpretations, is still to fall prey to the notion that the 'systematic' presentation of biblical truth, in modern philosophical or sociological garb, precedes and is a more advanced function than the *ad hoc* theological interpretation of biblical truth in confessional communities seeking to be faithful in their contemporary contexts.[22] Such a view still seeks to circumscribe the task of theology in terms of the classical notion of system. It fails adequately to appropriate a hermeneutical understanding of theology that takes into consideration the dynamic nature of the interpretive process with regard to both the text and the context.

It is my view that so-called systematic theology is best conceived of in hermeneutic rather than in systemic terms; that it is a discipline which must therefore be inextricably linked with the primary biblical pole in the hermeneutical process, as well as to the contemporary situation; and that it has a distinctive *translational* function that bridges the church's reflection on Scripture and its contemporary experience, reminding the church that Scripture is its canonical text.[23] Moreover, it has the primary hermeneutical function of articulating and clarifying the methods used to translate the message of Scripture into the church's particular cultural context. Here it clarifies and critiques the systematic whole within which the Bible is being interpreted. But one should not see its fundamental role as simply providing a system of theology that the church should adopt, anymore than one should view the role of biblical theology as providing a systematic summary of biblical thought, which can then be passed on to systematic theology for use in constructing a theological system for the church's use. So-called systematic theology must take more of a servanthood role than it is historically accustomed to, in assisting the church to be faithfully grounded in the gospel.

By the same token, if by biblical theology we simply mean a historical, descriptive discipline that needs to furnish the data for the task of systematic theology, then in a paradigm of theology as hermeneutics that descriptive function is not best described as 'theology' but as 'exegesis.' However, if biblical theology claims to be doing more than exegesis, and is in fact attempting to replace the inadequacy of systematic theology, then it has nonetheless moved into the interpretive tasks historically claimed by systematics, but only by another name.

But now, in addition, biblical theology suffers from an identity crisis, for it does not adequately know whether its task is primarily exegetical and descriptive or systematic and prescriptive in the larger hermeneutical sense. It seems that the modern hermeneutical context has placed biblical theology in a position where it cannot simply choose between the exegetical or the systematic role, but must clearly recognize a more full-orbed hermeneutical function for itself.

It is my view that the function we still describe as biblical theology is most adequately understood as representing one hermeneutical pole (anchored in the discipline of exegesis), and that it need not claim to replace systematics by another name. Rather, it should understand its own function as serving the broader task of theology as hermeneutics, moving between the text and the contemporary situation. But it should also understand itself as having a more particular role of reminding the broader theological endeavor—particularly as it is carried on in the social matrix of the church—of the primacy of the biblical, textual pole in hermeneutical understanding.

If, then, the functions of biblical and systematic theology are both conceptualized in a hermeneutical paradigm, the two disciplines are drawn into a different relationship with each other. They are not governed by a building-block model, where systematics builds on biblical theology; nor by a replacement model, where biblical theology assumes it can somehow replace the task of systematics, or systematics thinks it can somehow do without biblical theology; nor are they jointly governed by a reductionistic understanding of the task of theology based simply on a system-building or source-to-application model. Rather, they come to be closely related in an interactive model, or one configured in terms of concentric circles, where their fundamental goal and function are really the same, but the matrices and parameters governing their activity might be somewhat different, depending on the context in which the theological task takes place, and thus the purposes for which it is engaged.

In such a paradigm the question must be asked whether we should not then dispense with the old labels and give the various tasks—or this larger unitive task—a more appropriate name. It seems that the very labels we attach to the respective theological tasks militates against a more unitive understanding of the role of theology. There is a sense in which the rubric and practice of theology as hermeneutics has already tended to encompass and supercede some of the standard nomenclature. Yet at this juncture, it seems unlikely that the theological enterprise will quickly dispense with the standard labels and categories used to describe the various functions. Obviously, the classical designations for speaking about the theological task already have been significantly modified and redefined over time. And we must continue to be open to finding new ways of understanding, naming, and expressing the fundamental tasks accompanying the church's existence in the world. However, what is more important than changing labels is to bring our modes of thought and our ways of doing theology into conformity with the church's best current understanding of that task.

3. *Hermeneutical Theology and the Classical Models.* Under the current historical and cultural circumstances, it is clear that biblical understanding and the nature of theological reflection are at a critical juncture. For the shift that has taken place in this most recent contemporary paradigm is, in certain respects, more significant than the ones that occurred in the classical period. Although the classical paradigms—theology as knowledge, as science, and as practice—differed significantly in the central focus they gave to the task of theology, they were similar in this respect: they had a common definitional understanding of theology that was content-based. The classical paradigms instinctively understood that there was a specific content to be appropriated, understood, or applied. Furthermore, there was also significant agreement concerning the nature of the theological content, even after one allowed for all the traditional doctrinal differences.

However, in the contemporary paradigm of theology as hermeneutics a significant shift has occurred. First, the basic issues are approached on hermeneutical rather than on doctrinal grounds. The basic questions asked are not only questions pertaining to the necessity to appropriate divine knowledge, or the formulation of correct doctrine, or the translation and application of the doctrine into practice. Rather, the question is how one comes to appropriate theological understanding at all in one's particular context. How does one do this, taking seriously the biblical text, which represents the original and primary witness to the basic events informing theological understanding. Here

a strong emphasis is placed on process and context of theological formulations, and much less on the final product and content of doctrinal formulations.
Here the basic questions regarding the nature of biblical understanding and
theological reflection move behind the assumptions of the classical paradigms.

Second, the contemporary paradigm of theology as hermeneutics does not
necessarily assume a common doctrinal viewpoint to which this hermeneutical
understanding will lead. Conscious of the emerging postmodern context, it
accepts more readily the plurality of spiritualities, theologies, and strategies,
rather than pressing for an actual or perhaps even a potential, broadly based
agreement regarding theological or religious truth. Thus, the contemporary
paradigm of theology as hermeneutics has raised fundamental questions regarding the nature of biblical understanding and theological reflection. It has
done so hermeneutically, rather than doctrinally, with more of an emphasis on
context than on content. It focuses more on the process of discovering and
ascertaining truth in the context of religious pluralism, rather than on a final
doctrinal position that is acceptable to a broad hearing. It attempts to take
seriously the particularity of theological convictions.

Theology as hermeneutics has made a significant contribution to understanding the theological task by incorporating into that task the two
hermeneutical poles of the biblical text and our contemporary context. It has
done so by taking seriously the reality of pluralism in the modern world. In
its attempt to counter the modern reductionistic trends in theology, it has
reopened the question of the nature and task of theology at a more basic level.
However, with its strong focus on context instead of content, and process
instead of product, it has also tended to be open to criticism regarding its
theological ambiguity and incipient relativism. Does this paradigm play too
much into the pluralistic and relativistic language of late modernity?
Interestingly enough, this assessment has made some of the positive features of
the classical paradigm, by way of contrast, seem more viable again. In fact,
the bankruptcy of so many of our modern theological alternatives has led an
increasing number of contemporary theologians to look more carefully at the
classical models for theological resources.

In my earlier discussion of these classical paradigms I mainly attempted
to describe their development in their respective historical contexts, and their
historical demise as the next paradigm emerged. This has had the intended
effect of giving them a mainly critical assessment. It has perhaps also uninten-
tionally given the impression that these classical paradigms are not operative
in the contemporary world, or that in principle they should no longer inform
the contemporary church and theology. The fact is that, in the midst of the
emergent contemporary theological models, these classical models are in
varying degrees still operative in Christian communities today.[24]

Moreover, it would not accord with my intention to give the classical
paradigms only a critical reading, and by implication the contemporary
models mainly a positive one. Not only would that represent a faulty histori-

ography, but it would close the door to our need to have the past inform the present, even though it will always be reconstituted in a different context. Yet it must be noted that the future of theology does not lie in simply making undifferentiated appeals to the past. It must do so discerningly and with a great deal of sensitivity to context, both then and now. But contemporary theology must continually draw from the church's past in shaping its own framework. In principle, the hermeneutical paradigm allows for that, but in practice its bias tends at times to be against the constructive use of the past.

It is not within the realm of possibility to assess, in this essay, all the positive and negative features of each of the theological paradigms in their historical context. It is my conviction that the emergence and development of theology largely out of one social, historical or theological matrix has been a detrimental development in the church.[25] Theological reflection arose in the historical context of dominant western culture. It matured in the conceptual and institutional framework of authority, in the intellectual world of classical Christian orthodoxy. The critical question in our contemporary cross-cultural context of theological pluralism and relativism is whether theology can or must be disengaged from that classical framework; to what extent it is able to retrieve, translate, and thus build on that framework; and whether it can or should have a distinctively post-modern form. These are the deeper questions lingering behind the presenting problem of the relationship between biblical and systematic theology.

It is my conviction that it is possible and necessary within the contemporary context to construct working models that do not at the outset, or in principle, explicitly or implicitly, rule out the possibility of having these classical paradigms continue to inform us positively. Of course, one can never assume full continuity or complete discontinuity, but one must have some ongoing dialectical and hermeneutical relationship with past models, that is, with tradition. For theology as hermeneutics will not, in its best form, ignore classical tradition for the sake of contemporary translation, but will rather seek to do the latter in light of the former and, where possible, build on it.

Thus, to complete the analysis of theological paradigms, I am proposing a framework that draws its impetus from the concern of the contemporary hermeneutical model to define the theological task contextually, but which also appeals to the major strengths of the classical theological paradigms. Their quintessential understanding of the task of theology in its context must not be lost for ours, but must be appropriated critically and constructively within the emerging paradigms of our culture and our world.

I V
A Confessional Paradigm For Theology

F. Theology as Confession

Thesis: Theology, as a task grounded in the biblical narrative, is confessional language attending to a full-orbed hermeneutical understanding of God's presence in the context of a confessional community in the world.

As an outgrowth of the analytical framework developed so far, we are proposing an understanding of "theology as confession," a model which, by building discerningly on the contemporary hermeneutical model, is able critically and constructively to incorporate significant features from each of the classical historical models. I will attempt to build my case on both biblical-historical and contemporary-contextual grounds.[26] I begin with the biblical-historical pole of the hermeneutical process.

1. Hermeneutical Foundations: A Canonical Perspective. Central to this model is the notion of 'confession.' On this point, the New Testament is instructive. It reflects the apostolic church's confession of faith in a wide variety of ways. Beyond the lexical data surrounding the biblical concept of 'confession', it is particularly pertinent for our discussion to take note of the various confessions that are used in connection with the worship settings of the early church, related to baptism and the eucharist.[27] What do we make of these early christological confessions? How do they inform our theological model?

It is my thesis that the full-orbed concept of confession in the New Testament must be understood in terms of acts of worship, statements of doctrine, and the ongoing process of translating faith into life. This threefold unitive perspective relating to the modes, concepts, and practices of the early church expression of faith provides some initial biblical support for considering a model of theology as confession. Accordingly, the following observations need to be made.[28]

First, it is significant that, in the New Testament, the verb "to confess" (*exomologeo*) appears more frequently than the noun. Thus, in its original form confession is an event, an act that is a response to what God has done in and through Jesus Christ toward creating a confessing people. Consequently, in the New Testament all confession involves the joyous expression of gratitude to God for his presence in the believers' lives. That is why the early church as a resurrection community, in effect, does not *have* a confession; it *exists in* its confessing, in its response of faith-obedience to the servant lordship of Jesus Christ. Accordingly, confession in the early church finds its basic expression and response in the eschatologically celebrative statement: "Jesus Christ is Lord." Here we see confession expressed as worship. This was truly an expression of one's being in word and deed.

Second, it must also be noted that the oldest summaries of the early church's preaching revolve around the cross and resurrection. This is reflected, for example, in the elemental structure of the earliest forms of the apostolic sermonic material in the Acts of the Apostles: "you killed him, but God raised him from the dead." The early christological hymns are a foundational representation of this death/resurrection structure. Out of these stylized summations, hymnically expressed, there developed a body of distinctive doctrine held as a sacred trust from God. It was central to the apostolic preaching (kerygma) and teaching (didache). Doctrine in the early church was but another extension or expression of its preaching and teaching. Subsequent to the apostolic period, these basic doctrinal formulations went through a redaction process linked to the formation of the classical Christian creeds. For the New Testament church, confession involved the affirmation of true doctrine, an affirmation that was not without its struggle in the pluralistic context of Jewish and Greek culture.

Third, the New Testament concept of confession instinctively involved an understanding of living one's faith concretely. The notion of confession (*exomologeo*) is not only inextricably linked to the central concepts of *kerygmai* (to preach) and *didasko* (to teach), but also to *martureo* (to witness). The early church's confession involved an ongoing process of translating faith into life, frequently in the context of suffering. The force of the New Testament concept of confession includes a strong affirmation of the witnessing dimension. Implied in this is a clear apologetic that this person Jesus and no other is Christ the Lord. For early Christians this was not simply talk, but fundamentally a walk.

Stanley J. Samartha's comments are most apropos. He says that the church in its mission must press into service the concept of 'witness,' for "'witness'[*marturia*] is a biblical term" and together with 'kerygma' and 'diakonia' involves a "readiness to suffer and die for the sake of others, through which the Lordship of Christ is confessed." Therefore,

> witnessing to the Lordship of Jesus Christ cannot be mere verbal proclamation to the world at large. It has to be con-crete and particular in the living context of relationships. It is not just a statement to be accepted, but a confession to be made at the end, not at the beginning, of an experience.[29]

One final thing must be said regarding the New Testament understanding of confession. Confession here is first and foremost a corporate act and only derivatively an individual one. The very existence of the church depends on it. Because confession of faith in the biblical sense is a profoundly communal act, statement, and process of life, a confessing church discerningly listens to what others, past and present, have said. Our understanding of the theological task must always be shaped by this perspective. For this reason, contemporary theology must also listen carefully to voices from the classical past.

It is my contention that a New Testament understanding of the concept of confession provides adequate support for understanding theology as confession. To understand theology as confession on biblical grounds means that the task of theology is inextricably linked with a unitive understanding of confession as worship, doctrine, and life. It is involved in a holistic rendition of the Christian faith, inclusive of being, thinking, and doing. Thus, celebrating God's presence, thinking critically about the meaning of God in life, and acting obediently in response to God's will and way come into the orbit of theology. To define theology strictly as conceptual inquiry is simply too narrow a definition of the term and the task.

   2. Historical Framework: The Classical Paradigms. It is my conviction that understanding theology as confession provides the necessary framework into which one can critically incorporate central dimensions of each classical model. This paradigm serves as a heuristic devise to view the three classical models as each representing an integral part of a broader and deeper understanding of theology. Rather than seeing each model as having run its course and as no longer relevant, I am suggesting that theology as knowledge, as science, and as practice, properly understood, are all essential to the task of theology; but they have been pulled apart and separated from each other through the epochal shifts that have occurred in western culture.

   Moreover, I would suggest that the threefold classical development of theology as knowledge, science, and practice is roughly synonymous with the threefold canonical understanding of confession as worship, doctrine, and life. My purpose here is not to make a simple correlation between biblical themes and historical developments. But I am, in principle, suggesting that historical developments in the church frequently separate what is understood much more integratively in the scriptural context, and that the inadequacy of a particular historical development—for example, the reduction of theology to a narrow view of science—lies not so much with what is being emphasized as in the absence of the whole from which it has been separated. It is my view that much can be gained for our understanding of theology by retrieving the significant parts that have been separated, through historical development, from the whole of the theological task. I will attempt to do this briefly with each of the classical models.[30]

   First, the model of theology as knowledge stands as a constant reminder that theology must not lose its redemptive goal within the matrix of the church. In this model, the task of theology is closely connected with an understanding of Christian community as redemptive in nature and taking seriously its received confessional tradition and its truth convictions. Here theology is linked to the churchly tasks that center on the corporate and individual occurrences of redemption. Here theology as salvific and sapiential knowledge evokes understanding and action. It shapes one's experience of God and therefore one's self-understanding, identity and spiritual formation. This model reminds us that, in the historical matrix of the earlier Christian period, theology is done through worship, liturgy and story; that its confessional matrix is the creed that gives rise to first-order, liturgical language; and that as confession, it functions expressively in the public sphere as doxology.

Today, the Christian tradition that continues persistently to remind us of this indispensable dimension of theology is the Eastern Orthodox Church, largely as a suffering minority in the eastern context of Islam and atheistic Communism. As Demetrios J. Constantelos writes, "The Orthodox have viewed religion as the right 'doxa,' and 'doxa' means glory, glorification. Thus Orthodoxy is not so much right creed as right doxology-worship of God the Creator." Thus, "worship in the early church meant, as it does in modern Orthodoxy, the centrality of Christ in the Eucharist, in faith, life, and action." This is the Orthodox model of theology and discipleship.[31] The twentieth-century charismatic movement has also provided various manifestations of a doxological model of theology throughout the global Christian community.

Second, the model of theology as science stands as a reminder that theology must not lose its goal of enabling the Christian community by interpreting the church's doctrinal tradition in relation to its contemporary situation. Here theology as a discipline, unified in its theological character and subject matter, is involved in scholarly inquiry, seeking consistency and coherence, in the matrix of sound theological teaching. Here theology is rigorously involved in ascertaining the truth. Here it develops the content, meaning, and parameters of Christian confession. It directs us to ultimate reality and promotes seeing that reality as God's reality, attempting to bring our minds, through critical thinking, in conformity with that reality. This model reminds us that in the historical matrix of the medieval Christian period theology focused significantly on words, language, and statements; that its confessional matrix is doctrine that represents second-order, analytical language; and that as confession, it functions descriptively in the public sphere as doctrine. Today, the major Christian traditions that have consistently reminded us of this indispensable dimension of theology are the western Roman Catholic and particularly the conservative Protestant traditions, as dominant, established traditions in the western cultural context of secular humanism.

Third, the model of theology as practice stands as a reminder that theology must not lose its fundamentally practical character and goal of attending to the life, existence, and behavior of the believer, or the faith community in the world. This model reminds us that theology is inextricably linked with Christian experience in the matrix of society. In the strongest representations of this model, the authenticity and integrity of theology are seen to be preserved only through the costly practice of Christian discipleship in the world. For it affirms that discipleship behavior changes reality, and that it constrains one to reflect faithfully on the servant lordship of Jesus Christ.

This model also reminds us that theology is not primarily an activity limited to the professional clergy and theologians, but is fundamentally an activity in which all of God's people can, and indeed must, participate in the context of their life-situations. It reminds us that corporate and personal insight without technical scholarship can also be theological reflection. It reminds us that the theology is not primarily theoretical in nature but fundamentally practical knowledge, promoting, forming, and disciplining theological understanding for faithful witness in the world.[32] This model reminds us that in the modern Christian period, theology has focused significantly on life, witness, ethics and the contemporary situation; that its confessional matrix is the practice of Christian life in the world, which is, in effect, first-order language (language of worship) in an ethical key; and that as confession, it functions prescriptively in the public sphere as discipleship. Today, the major Christian traditions that most radically remind us of this indispensable dimension of theology are the two-thirds world Christians who are an oppressed minority in the southern hemisphere, countries frequently dominated by the political and economic powers of the North. Earlier, the classical liberal Protestant tradition gave significant expression to the ethical and practical dimensions of Christian faith and theology, in the context of an increasingly modern and secular western culture.

Again, it is important to reiterate that our purpose is to establish a hermeneutically sound and historically sensitive model of theology. Here I have contended that not only do each of the classical paradigms, within their historical matrices, remind us of an integral dimension of the theological task, but that these dimensions are inextricably linked in a more full-orbed understanding of the theological task. They are important, separated parts belonging to a more unitive whole that I have named theology as confession. The temptation, of course, will be to try to associate each of these three areas with a scholarly discipline via the encyclopedia model—biblical, systematic, and practical theology. But this is only to retreat, once again, into a reductionistic concept of theology, and away from a hermeneutically sound and historically sensitive model. My claim is that all three of these dimensions must be held together in a full-orbed understanding of the nature and function of theology. Worship, word, and witness must be inseparably connected in carrying out the complete hermeneutical task of a confessional community in the world. Theology as confession represents a 'thick description' of that task. It reveals the depth and richness of the theological task and keeps it from being reduced to a single, timeless essence.

3. *Heuristic Formulations: A Contemporary Proposal.* (a) Confession as Transformative Language. So far, I have based my claims regarding theology as confession on biblical and historical grounds. It also will be necessary to establish my case more fully in the context of contemporary hermeneutical thought. This will provide the conceptual grounds that permit holding together

the dimensions of act, statement, and the ongoing processing of life. Within the framework of contemporary hermeneutics and epistemology, I believe that 'confession' is best conceptualized in terms of a speech-act model of language. Such a view of language engenders a full-orbed understanding of confession, namely, that it also creates reality rather than simply defines reality.[33]

In this view theology as 'confession' is understood as a "statement" or a "locution" employed in a particular kind of act, a speech-act, which aims at expressing and producing "life." It is language understood in terms of how it is used and what it does.[34] In other words, 'confession' is language understood as speech-act, where statements as locutions are employed as an act with the aim of expressing and producing life, and where linguisticality is defined by the full-orbed meaning of a speaking and listening God (*dabar/logos*) who acts and responds in the "language" of being, thinking, and doing.[35] Thus, "theology as confession" is what the church, in its hermeneutical reflection on Scripture, "says" about God in terms of act, statement, and process of life. This conceptual framework, in my estimation, is able to accommodate the integrative biblical understanding of confession as an act of worship, a statement of doctrine, and the process of living faithfully. Likewise, it provides a structure by which we can critically integrate the classical options of theology as knowledge, as science, and as practice.

Theology as confession is "language" that does not only describe reality, it also creates reality. It does not just state what the church believes, it gives shape to its faith by constructing a new reality by attending to Christian confession as worship, word, and witness. But we cannot make this profound claim for theology apart from grounding it in its primary context, which is Scripture as the primary witness to the apostolic faith. This witness is confessionally embodied in the early Christian communities and continually transforms them. Thus, the Bible itself, in a fundamental sort of way, needs to be construed as a primary 'confession' in terms of a speech-action or text-action model. Here Scripture as confession not only bears witness to a new reality, but is itself continuously taken up in the church's interpretive process, through which it repeatedly gives birth to new spiritual and social reality.

This understanding of Scripture as a kind of original confession presupposes the importance of a community of faith that confesses that the God of the biblical story performs reality changing actions—transformative actions—in and through the church's faithful construal of Scripture. The church's act of confessing the truth of the biblical witness, in its particular context, is a profoundly transformative function, and it is my contention that the task of theology must emerge out of the heart of that transforming function.

Therefore, theology as confession in worship, word, and witness designates the community's and the individual's orientation to God and to the world. This unitive, threefold dimension carries with it the affective and interactional dimensions of reality, and does not slant the theological task only to a cognitive/analytical or a pragmatic/functional framework. It must avoid the excesses of both an objectivistic ontologism and a subjectivistic pragmatism. Theology as worship, word, and witness within the confessional paradigm intrinsically relates to the reality of God, the people of God, and the world. It is a transformative hermeneutical process grounded in a historico-relational ontology.[36] Thus theology as transformative, confessional language does not reduce the theological task to a hermeneutical process or an epistemological formulation, but grounds it ontologically within transformative reality of a God who "speaks" and "listens" in and through the experience, explanation, and expression of confessing communities of faith.

(b) Confession as Embodied Language. However, the focus of theology as confession is not just on how the divine acts transformatively in the human sphere (more so the classical theology emphasis), but also on how the human arena experiences the divine activity of God (more so the contemporary theological emphasis). These two spheres of reality must not be separated dualistically. It is my view that the three inseparable dimensions of the confessional paradigm are also eminently translatable into the sphere of concrete human experience of God in the world. It is therefore important to understand human experience of divine reality in terms of our analytical grid of confession as worship, word, and witness.[37] First, there is the level of "basic experience," which refers to the immediate experience of God's presence in personal or corporate Christian experience, in a sense uninterpreted. This would be the first-order level of worship as experienced in personal and corporate ways in the gathered experience of God's people.

Second, there is the level of "formed experience," which is experience as conveyed in and through the cultural "language" of one's context. This is first-order language transposed into another key, namely, the actual experiential, embodied witness and ministry of God's people in the world. It is always expressed through the language of culture.

Third, there is the level of "interpreted experience," which is the systematic attempt to think about and integrate spiritual and religious experience into a larger world view. This would be the second-order level of confession as word, where the church attempts to articulate coherently and consistently, and to validate, its faith in its cultural context.

This portrayal of the paradigm in terms of the language of human experience focuses the common distinction in theology between first-order and second-order language—that is, the primary language of experience versus the secondary language of reflection. It is my view that the content given to first-order language in the classical and contemporary models of theology is deeply influenced by the interiority of western spirituality, and especially of contemporary western devotion. However, within the framework of the confessional paradigm, first-order language is significantly expanded and indeed transposed into another key. Here it still remains first-order language—that is, the language of primary faith-experience—but it moves beyond corporate or individual devotional language (confession as worship) to integrate and embody the experience of the church reaching out beyond itself in discipleship, mission, service, action, and ethics (confession as witness, or worship in its full-orbed New Testament sense of worship as service).

There is a real sense in which first-order language must be transposed into a key that includes the entire sphere of the church's experience of embodying God's presence in her public witness in the world. This is truly the range of New Testament first-order language.[38] This is not language "about" our experience of God. This is first-order language of the experience of God's presence as witness in and to the world. This is first-order experiential language, in terms of both the inward and the outward journey of spirituality and formation. It entails the embodiment of a transformative witness to the world, grounded in the ontological and experiential reality of God's presence. Therefore, the concept of first-order language has to be greatly expanded and theologically grounded. First-order language must be inclusive of worship and witness. The confessional paradigm attempts to do this.[39]

It is also the case that second-order language is profoundly influenced by modern, western notions of rationality and language. Just as first-order language tends to be run through the epistemological grid of an emotive-expressivist view of language (and thus excessively subjectivistic), so second-order language is largely understood through the epistemological grid of a propositional/cognitivist view of language (and is thus excessively objectivistic). The epistemological framework of our model of theology as confession helps to transcend the limitation of these views. Here second-order language is not so much "a set of propositions to be believed," but is more "the medium in which one moves, a set of skills that one employs in living one's life."[40]

This view of language can relate second-order language much more integratively to first-order language, so that the task of theology can incorporate both levels. Second-order language represents the reflexive action of thought on the inward and outward processes of believers' experiences in the world. Theology as confession embraces and embodies this entire experiential-reflexive process.

Therefore, my central thesis is that theology, as a task grounded in the biblical narrative, is confessional language attending to a full-orbed hermeneutical understanding of God's transformative presence embodied in confessional communities in the world. Theology as confession attends to worship as the primary language of faith, to word of doctrine as the essential grammar of faith, and to the process of witness in life as the indispensable task of testing the adequacy of this confessional language and grammar and continually shaping it. It must do this in the twofold context of the biblical narrative and the contemporary community of faith. The task of theology involves attending to the full range of this transformative and embodied hermeneutical process.[41]

V
Conclusion

It is my contention that a model of theology as confession permits a broader and deeper understanding of the nature and role of theology. It can hermeneutically appropriate the primacy of the biblical witness from the very outset of the theological task; it can discerningly incorporate important features from the classical models of theology; and it can critically appropriate the strengths of contemporary models, and interact genuinely with the contemporary situation.

Theology as confession is a model that makes exegesis of the biblical text (and the contemporary context) a precondition for theological reflection, and theological reflection an indispensible horizon for such exegesis. Simultaneously, it is a model that affirms the transformative function of the theological task, which must always be embodied in its present context. Thus, theology as confession attempts to be historically sensitive and hermeneutically sound. It seeks to appropriate a full-orbed understanding of the theological task. Without such vision, the church and theology will continue to be pulled back into the historical conundrums, and imprisoned in the contemporary hermeneutical crises.

Notes

1   Hans Küng, *Theology for the Third Millennium: An Ecumenical View* (New York: Doubleday Books, 1988), 1-11. See also Howard John Loewen, "The Mission of Theology," *Explorations of Systematic Theology from Mennonite Perspectives*, OP, 7 (Elkhart: Institute of Mennonite Studies, 1984), 84-88.

2   Küng, Theology for the Third Millennium, 11.

3   Ibid., 6.

4   Gerhard Ebeling, *The Study of Theology* (Philadelphia: Fortress Press, 1978), 1.

5   Edward Farley, Theologia: The Fragmentation and Unity of Theological Education (Philadelphia: Fortress Press, 1983), 32.

6   Jack B. Rogers and Donald K. McKim, *The Authority and Interpretation of Scripture* (San Francisco: Harper & Row, 1979), 15. This work is particularly useful in analyzing the way in which Scripture was understood and used as an authority in theology in the various periods of the western church. I am using it, together with works by Wolfhart Pannenber and Edward Farley, to develop the basic classical models of theology.

7   Farley, *Theologia*, 29-48.

8   Ibid., 33.

9   Rogers and McKim, *Authority of Scripture*, 12.

10   Wolfhart Pannenberg, *Theology and the Philosophy of Science* (Philadelphia: Westminster Press, 1976), 349-352. Since I will make frequent reference to the works of Pannenberg, Rogers and McKim, and Farley (see notes 5 and 6), I will hereafter refer to them in the text, by authors' names.

11   It is important and instructive to understand Augustine's use of Scripture within the context of the authority of church and creed, and in relationship to his view of the interiorty of knowledge. See Howard John Loewen, "The Use of Scripture in Augustine's Theology," *SJT* 34 (1979): 201-224.

12   Susan J. Hekman, *Hermeneutics and the Sociology of Knowledge* (South Bend: University of Notre Dame Press, 1986), 139-159.

13   Earlier, hermeneutics had a text-based focus which was then expanded to include epistemological and ontological issues. Today, hermeneutics, as philosophical hermeneutics, "investigates the relationship of human understanding to the interpretation of texts, as well as to the so-called 'text analogues' of human language and society" (Mark I. Wallace, "The World of the Text: Theological Hermeneutics in the Thought of Karl Barth and Paul Ricoeur" [Ph.D. diss., University of Chicago, 1986], 2. See now Wallace's *The Second Naivete: Barth, Ricoeur, and the New Yale Theology*, SABH, 6 (Macon, GA: Mercer University Press, 1990. My references will be to Wallace's unpublished dissertation).

14   Charles M. Wood, *The Formation of Christian Understanding: An Essay in Theological Hermeneutics* (Philadelphia: Fortress Press, 1981), 15-29.

15   Ibid., 20.

16   Werner G. Jeanrond, *Text and Interpretation as Categories of Theological Thinking* (New York: Crossroad, 1988), chapter 1.

17   Quoted in ibid., 130.

18   Ibid., 134.

19   Ibid., 147.

20   Ibid., 140-142.

21   Ibid., 139.

22   See ibid., ch 3, and Wallace, "The World of the Text," ch 6.

23   Loewen, "The Mission of Theology," 88-97.

24   We find a good illustration of this in Robert K. Johnston, ed., *The Use of the Bible in Theology: Evangelical Options* (Atlanta: John Knox Press, 1985). One can find the various classical and contemporary paradigms represented within this broad and most useful representation of specifically evangelical uses of Scripture in theology.

25   Here I agree with Farley's assessment throughout his work, that the development of theology in the western tradition has taken a "fatal" turn.

26   Thomas N. Finger in his two volume work on *Christian Theology: An Eschatological Approach* (Scottsdale: Herald Press, 1987, 1989) develops eschatologically oriented systematic theology in terms of the dynamic relationship between the kerygmatic and the apologetic poles of the theological task. He

shows unusual sensitivity to both the biblical text and the contemporary context in his hermeneutical understanding of the task of theology.

27   The following texts, either implicitly or explicitly, express the christologically centered confession of the early church: John 1:1-14; Rom. 1:3-4, 6:17, 10:9f; 1 Cor. 8:6, 11:23-26, 12:3, 15:3-5, 15:22; Phil. 2:5-11; Eph. 2:14-16, 4:6, 5:19; Col. 1:15-20, 2:6, 3:16; 1 Thess. 1:9f, 2:6; 2 Thess. 2:15; 1 Tim. 3:16, 2:5, 4:6, 6:12-16; 2 Tim. 1:13-14; Heb. 1:3, 3:1, 4:14, 6:1f, 10:23; 1 Pet. 3:18-22; 1 John 1:9, 2:23, 4:2, 4:15.

28   Howard John Loewen, "A Confessing People," *Direction* 15 (1986), 22-23. In this essay, I am relying on that body of recent biblical scholarship that has provided the new perspectives on the early church confessions as understood in the context of baptism and/or the eucharist; as expressed in the earliest christological hymns; and as related to the central New Testament concepts of kerygma (proclamation), didache (teaching), marturia (witness), etc.

29   "The Lordship of Jesus Christ and Religious Pluralism," in *Christ's Lordship & Religious Pluralism,* ed. G. H. Anderson and T. F. Stransky (New York: Orbis Books, 1981), 34.

30   Such an approach is taken by George A. Lindbeck, who in his cultural-linguistic model takes up and accommodates the positive features of both the propositional-cognitivist and the experiential-expressivist models, which in other ways he finds seriously deficient. See especially chapter 2 of *The Nature of Doctrine: Religion and Theology in a Postliberal Age* (Philadelphia: Westminster Press, 1984). It is also significant to note the correlation between the three paradigms under discussion in Lindbeck and the three classical paradigms of theology as knowledge, as science, and as practice. An implication of this correlation is that the first model—theology as knowledge—is better able to accommodate the other two than either of them is able to accommodate the others.

31   "An Orthodox Perspective," in Christ's Lordship and Religious Pluralism, 189-90.

32   Those who understand the theological task in terms of this model find it difficult to affirm constructs that define theology and religion primarily in terms of the theoretical. Schreiter describes it well. He says that "Christianity's giving predominance to religion as a view of life rather than a way of life cannot be traced to Jesus or the New Testament as such." He asks, "Why did the view of life come to predominate over the way of life in Christianity." And, "Why are ideas so important to us? What does this emphasis on ideas say about our pastoral experience of community in the Lord Jesus Christ?" For Schreiter the issue of theology today "has as much to do with the state of our communities and our sense of belonging as it does with our formulation of ideas" (Robert J. Schreiter, "Response," in *Christ's Lordship and Religious Pluralism,* 49-51).

33   I am indebted here to George A. Lindbeck's cultural-linguistic approach, as articulated in *The Nature of Doctrine.* In place of the current, dominant theories governing religion and theology—propositionalist-cognitivist and experiential-expressivist—Lindbeck proposes a cultural-linguistic ap-

proach characterizing the human sciences. In this interpretive scheme, religion, doctrine, and theology are understood "as comprehensive interpretive schemes, usually embodied in . . . narratives," which when used make possible "the description of realities, the formulation of beliefs," and the experience of inner convictions instilled and shaped by "becoming skilled in the language, the symbol system of a given religion (32-34). There is a significant correlation between the three implied levels in Lindbeck's model and my understanding of theology as confession in the threefold terms of worship, word, and witness. Wallace represents a similar approach. He states that "theological hermeneutics is the interpretive method by which the language-event of the Word of God is understood in the present." Following Barth and Ricoeur, he says that "the event of the Word of God witnessed to in the biblical texts is the subject matter of theological hermeneutics," which is "more than the methodology of exegesis," for "it concerns the constitution of the theological object as 'speech event'." It is "the understanding of 'words' as present-day 'events' of revelation that characterizes hermeneutical inquiry." Thus "the subject matter of hermeneutics is not the biblical texts as such, but these texts as occasions for the word-event of God speaking to us again in the present" (Wallace, "The World of the Text," 86).

34 I am indebted in this section to Jerry Truex, my research assistant, for the further clarification he has brought to my position through his analysis of speech-act theory and its application to an understanding of theology as confession, especially in his research paper "Christian Faith: A Non-foundational Exploration and Proposal" (Fresno, California: Mennonite Brethren Biblical Seminary, December, 1989).

35 See the following note.

36 Analytically speaking, hermeneutics is a function of one's epistemology, which is grounded in one's prior ontological understanding of the way in which God's reality is known in the church and in the world. It is instructive to see the kinds of hermeneutics that emerge from the different constructs of the relationship between God, the people of God, and the world, and how the nature of the theological task is construed in light of each construct. My focus has deliberately been on the hermeneutical, yet with a concern for its ontological grounding. We have not tried to create another ontotheological system seeking to ground theology on the basis of a general philosophical scheme that tries to be more exact than the church's first and second order languages. We agree with Wallace that "whenever theology is hermeneutically sensitive to the surplus of meaning always present in the Bible's competing modes of discourse, it will remain suspicious of any philosophical and conceptual terminology that offers one-to-one equivalents to Scripture's diverse ways of speaking." Yet this suspicion "should not issue in hostility toward the disciplined use of extratheological concepts and vocabulary in Christian reflection." For "hermeneutical theology is not a species of philosophical theology, but it is not simply exegesis either." Its interpretive function is by nature ad hoc and will also involve "the cautious use of extra-theological language" (Wallace, "The World of the Text," 272-275.)

37   See Arnold Bittlinger, ed, The Church is Charismatic: The World Council of Churches and the Charismatic Movement (Geneva: World Council of Churches, 1982), 33-35.

38   Such an understanding is grounded christologically. As Costas puts it: The key to Jesus' authority "was not in his words but in the fact that these words were 'embodied in his presence.' His words were an extension of himself and he was filled with the presence of the Spirit of God" (Orlando E. Costas, "A Radical Evangelical Contribution From Latin America," in *Christ's Lordship and Religious Pluralism*, 138).

39   Lindbeck argues that a cultural-linguistic model transposes the experiential-expressivist emphasis on internalized first-order language into externalized dimensions from which the inner experience is derivative. In this interpretive scheme religion, doctrine, and theology as 'language' give shape and intensity to the the first-order language of inner experience (*Nature of Doctrine*, 34). Therefore, philosophically speaking, Lindbeck believes that it is unnecessary to conclude that 'first intentions' (those acts whereby we mentally attend to an activity) are somehow linguistically unstructured. For they are shaped by our reflective acts, that is our 'second intentions' (those acts whereby we reflect on our first intentions; p. 38).

40   Lindbeck, *Nature of Doctrine*, 38. Significantly, Lindbeck says that the second-order language of doctrines as rules involves propositions, but they are propositions expressing convictions about how first-order thought and language work. Accordingly, doctrines may function as a first-order proposition if so employed (ibid., 80).

41   Our thesis echoes James Wm. McClendon's understanding of the the theological task. He states, "Theology is the discovery, understanding, and transformation of the convictions of a convictional community, including the discovery and critical revision of their relation to one another and to whatever else there is." McClendon understands theology to be hermeneutical theology that is communally based by the hermeneutical vision of a shared awareness of the present Christian community as the primitive community and the eschatological community (*Systematic Theology: Ethics* [Abingdon Press, 1985], 31). Accordingly, there are also significant parallels between McClendon's understanding of ethics in terms of the three interrelated strands of the organic, the communal, and the anastatic, and my claim that the hermeneutical task of theology must be understood in terms of worship, word, and witness.

Chapter 7

Biblical and Systematic Theology
Constructing a Relationship

Ben C. Ollenburger

"Theology seems to be what theologians have been doing and will do. Possibly this tautology is a definition."[1]

I
Introduction

We would have an easier time relating biblical and systematic theology if we agreed on what we were relating. The issue this essay addresses is complicated by—perhaps it is constituted by—the lack of a consensus about what biblical theology is, or about what biblical theologians should do; the lack is hardly less serious in systematic theology. For that reason, we cannot simply point to the definition of biblical theology, and to that of systematic theology, and then propose some way of relating these two disciplines.[2] To speak of the relation between them without defining them would beg the question, and it would be a distraction. In any event, an account of the relation between biblical and systematic theology can only be in the form of a proposal about both. If we want a relationship between them, we will have to construct one. The proposal I will make in this essay is itself theological in nature; in other words, it is an argument that depends on theological grounds, and on a particular definition of systematic theology.[3] It is also a purely formal proposal that omits a host of material questions. Since one crucial test of any such a proposal is its usefulness in relation to Scripture itself, this one remains incomplete.[4]

In the following section of this essay, I will make some brief, historically oriented comments on the relation of biblical and systematic theology. This historical orientation seems essential, since many of the problems we face are the legacy of particular historical developments. In the third and fourth sections, I will discuss some of those problems, and particularly James Barr's

111

criticisms of biblical theology. This discussion will provide an opportunity for locating our specific issue—the relation of biblical and systematic theology—in the larger context of theology's relation to Scripture, and for defining that context more precisely. If things go as planned, this will clear the way for my own proposal in a fifth section.

I I
A Historical Diagnosis

Whatever may be the problems in defining their current relationship, biblical theology had its origin, and has had the greater part of its history, in relation to systematic or dogmatic theology, which is to say, in relation to specifically Christian theology.[5] Such a statement shows that I am talking about biblical theology as an area of inquiry and not merely as, for example, the theological content of the biblical books. If we were to limit the term to this latter meaning—to "the theology contained in the Bible," as it is often put—our question would be very different. Then we would be asking how contemporary theology, of whatever kind, related itself to the Bible's theology. It is not necessary now to go into the various reasons why we should not limit ourselves to this question, even if it should be an intelligible and legitimate question. It is sufficiently clear that if we can ask about the *history* of biblical theology, and say that it began approximately in the seventeenth century, then we are not talking only about the Bible's theology.

Something called biblical theology first emerged in the seventeenth century, around the time of the Thirty Years War (1618-1648). That historical conjunction may be more than coincidental. The war's havoc affected generations. Among its other, collateral effects, it cemented confessional divisions and hampered the distribution of Bibles. Some Protestant pastors owned no Bibles and had none available to them. At the war's end, there were no Bible's for sale at the Leipzig book fair, the largest book market in Europe. At the same time, bitter arguments between Lutherans and the Reformed in Protestant northern Germany constituted a further impoverishment of religious life. A return to the Bible promised to ameliorate those disputes while simultaneously providing a proof of Protestant Christianity against Roman Catholicism in southern Germany.[6] It is not surprising that, in such a context, the earliest expressly biblical theology was a polemical Protestant undertaking to demonstrate, against Roman Catholic teaching, that Scripture is the sufficient source and criterion of theology and doctrine.[7]

Biblical theology as a critique of doctrine was then very soon applied to Protestant theology itself. Protestant theology's formal dependence on the Bible meant that it was always open, in principle, to such critique. At the same time, the highly developed Protestant systems of theology were vulnerable to the charge, whether justified or not, that they were in some respect or another insufficiently biblical.[8] Biblical theology in the eighteenth century was not less interested in doctrine than were the scholastic theologians it criticized. It sought to reform theology on the basis of a thoroughly Protestant foundation, which would result in doctrines that were properly biblical. The pietistic impulses behind biblical theology in the early eighteenth century[9] were followed by rationalistic ones in its later years. For example, the young C. F. Ammon proposed to study the Bible in order to determine, according to the criterion of reason, which church doctrines needed to be reformed and which needed to be abandoned.[10]

While pietism and its version of biblical theology flourished in many parishes, the new biblical criticism spawned by an invigorated academic theology joined a new religious sensibility brought about by the spreading Enlightenment. The historical consciousness that emerged from these sources created yet another dissatisfaction with traditional theology, which was seen to be out of touch both with the historical character and religious vitality of the Bible, and with the religious needs of the churches. Within this intellectual and religious environment, Johann Philipp Gabler argued for a clear distinction between dogmatic and biblical theology.[11] Current discussions sometimes overlook that biblical theology had a history prior to Gabler; he did not invent it. Gabler's invention was to define biblical theology as something methodologically distinct from, but at the same time foundational to, dogmatic theology. Gabler intended this distinction, which soon assumed a life of its own, to provide a firm biblical basis—or, as he put it, a foundation in truth[12]— for dogmatics, and to make the latter more pertinent to the religious life of the churches. By the late nineteenth century, the dynamic, historical character of the Bible was again pitted against dogmatic theology. The history of religion school reacted against the dogmatic tradition in favor of a thoroughly critical and often romanticist historicism, which stressed an immediate encounter with the spirit of the biblical authors.[13]

The twentieth century dissatisfaction with liberal theology was indirectly related to the history of religion school, but turned against it with a vengeance. On this continent, the efforts of the biblical theology movement (beginning in the 1940s) to bring theology into closer relation with its biblical foundation were, once again, religiously motivated, attending both to the use of the Bible in the Christian churches and their theology, and to matters of academic responsibility.[14] That movement eroded on both fronts. In North America, theology progressively repudiated the neo-orthodox theological framework of the biblical theology movement, while critical study of the Bible uncovered its internal inconsistencies. Even those theologians and biblical scholars with neo-orthodox commitments found the movement to be misguided. As a result of these developments and others, including the emergence of various liberation theologies and a revitalized liberal theology, the relation of theology to the Bible is again an open question.

This may seem the appropriate place in the narrative to predict that bibli-cal theology will emerge in yet another form, as a critical response to recent developments in systematic theology. The prediction would be premature, however. This very brief overview is sufficient only to show that, throughout its history, biblical theology has had a close and a critical relation to systematic theology. Indeed, in each of its principal historical moments, it has emerged in critical response to—at least among other things—then current trends in systematic theology. But it emerged in different forms. For example, the biblical theology of the seventeenth century was not much different from the systematic theology against which biblical theology protested in the eighteenth and especially in the nineteenth century. This tendency of biblical and sys-tematic theology to coalesce should not be surprising, because, until relatively recent times, biblical and systematic theologians were not only working to-gether in the same faculties and departments, they were the same people. It was often the case, until late in the nineteenth century, that biblical theology was an inquiry undertaken by Christian theologians in order to reform or to reconceive systematic theology, and to provide its foundations.[15]

If our starting point were the Reformation, rather than the date when books with "biblical theology" in their title first appeared,[16] the picture would be quite different. Calvin's *Institutes of the Christian Religion* was in-tended as a handbook to guide Christian readers of the Bible, and Melanchthon's *Loci Communes* was first a set of explanatory comments to his lectures on St. Paul's Epistle to the Romans. In relation to the predominant Roman Catholic theology of their era, these works—leave alone those of Luther—can be seen as efforts in biblical theology. Indeed, Richard Muller speaks in this regard of the "Reformation...demand for a *biblical theology* responsive to the needs of piety and worship," a critical demand that "had ample precedent in the late Middle Ages."[17] On the other hand, in relation to developing Protestant theology—or even in relation to their own subsequent editions—the *Institutes* and the *Loci* can be taken as initial Protestant efforts in systematic theology. This complex situation makes it difficult, and perhaps pointless, to debate whether Calvin and, early on, Melanchthon were engaged in biblical or in systematic theology. It may be that the conditions of such a debate were already in place with the later editions of Melanchthon's text, or—in quite a different context—even earlier, when commentators on Peter Lombard's *Sentences*, in the fourteenth century, began to pay less attention to Scripture than to philosophy.[18] In any case, the possibility of such a debate depends, historically, on at least these conditions: (a) that some theology's appropriate relation to the Bible is crucially at issue; (b) that there are some criteria of appropriateness. Whatever those criteria may be, they are not abstractly fixed. The history of biblical theology's relation to systematic theology—or the history of theology itself—shows that those criteria have to be worked out concretely and afresh in different contexts. But if there are no such criteria, even in principle, or if they do not matter, then the relation of biblical to systematic theology can only ever be a historical question.

This abbreviated survey also helps to illustrate the point made in the introductory section, above. Taken in the abstract, the question, "What is the relation between biblical theology and systematic theology?" is only a distraction. That helps to explain why answers to this question typically beg it.

III
Scripture's Problematic Relation to Theology

A. HIstorical Criticism and the Independence of Biblical Theology

The preceding section of this essay has tried to show that the critical (and occasionally constructive) relation between biblical and systematic theology has largely turned on this question: What is the appropriate relation of theology to Scripture? Biblical theology as a particular area of inquiry, and perhaps as a discipline, has tended to raise a distinctive voice when that relation, exemplified in some current systematic theology, has been judged inappropriate on some grounds. With the development of biblical studies as a historical discipline, pursued in sometimes self-conscious independence of theology,[19] the issues became much more complex. Biblical (or Old or New Testament) theology continued to regard itself as important to systematic theology, but it grew increasingly reluctant or unable to say precisely *in what way*.

In place of an understanding, or an account, of how the two independent subjects—biblical and systematic theology—should be related, biblical theologians substituted the image of a transaction. This image, originating in the early years of the nineteenth century, has persisted—the image of biblical theology as a historical-critical inquiry whose results are passed on to systematic theologians for elaboration.[20] The image of a transaction that occurs between historians and theologians is sometimes perpetuated under the formula of "what it meant," in distinction from "what it means." It is not necessary to examine this formula in detail.[21] It is sufficient to say that the formula, with the transactional image it is sometimes used to capture, is itself unhelpful and has never accurately conveyed the relation of biblical to systematic theology.[22] Systematic theology is not now, nor has it ever been, simply the elaboration—perhaps with certain philosophical tools that only theologians possess—of what biblical scholars happen to discover in their theologically disinterested, purely historical research.[23]

In the past, biblical theology depended on the pertinence of a certain question, a question concerning the appropriateness of some theology's relation to Scripture. Obviously, *if* biblical theology is now conceived as a discipline or a specialty area wholly within historical-critical scholarship, then it cannot depend on the pertinence of that question.[24] Indeed, if it is principled, it cannot even take that question into account. It does not follow necessarily that biblical theology so conceived is then irrelevant either to Christian faith or specifically to systematic theology. Nor does it follow necessarily that biblical theology as a specialty area within historical-critical scholarship, or perhaps within the scientific study of religion (*Religionswissenschaft*), must remain ignorant of its possible relation to Christian faith or to systematic theology.[25] We can leave such arguments aside; it is sufficient to say that the question concerning the appropriateness of some theology's relation to Scripture cannot be pertinent to biblical theology so conceived. In this disciplinary realignment, both matters are left entirely to systematic theology. Systematic theologians must decide how or whether theology is appropriately related to Scripture, and only systematic theologians can judge how or whether biblical theology may be related to their work.

However we may evaluate this development, it represents a change in the role and self-understanding of biblical theology. Formerly, whenever the question was raised about the appropriateness of some theology's relation to Scripture, the answer always and necessarily included a proposal about the way in which historical-critical interpretation of the Bible becomes theologically useful.[26] If biblical theology now excludes that question in principle, reserving it to systematic theology, it may be unclear whether historical-critical interpretation of the Bible is in any sense a theological task, or whether it has a relation to theology. This was already at issue in the biblical theology movement, which criticized the lack of theological interest and usefulness in the then current interpretation of the Bible.

In its effort to redress matters as it saw them, it may be that the biblical theology movement was, in theory or in practice, susceptible of Edward Farley's criticism. "Biblical theology" he says, "is caught between the recognition that it is a historical undertaking—the uncovering of a 'theological' stratum of an ancient literature—and the pretension that the undertaking somehow establishes the truth of the theological contents uncovered."[27] While it seems unlikely—it seems incredible—that any contemporary biblical theologian would consider her "undertaking" itself to establish the truth of Scripture's content,[28] Farley's criticism at least points to an important issue. However we should define biblical theology, in what sense is it now theological? The definition of biblical theology as a historical-critical discipline first prompted this question; however, the question does not depend on that definition, or on the predominant use of historical-critical methods in biblical studies.[29] The question of biblical theology's *theological* character is crucial in any event; it is one that James Barr has addressed persistently. It may help to make the discussion more concrete, and it will provide me the opportunity to introduce some constructive points of my own, if we engage Barr in conversation.[30]

B. The Bible and Theology

In a recent essay, "Exegesis as a Theological Discipline Reconsidered and the Shadow of the Jesus of History,"[31] Barr poses the following question: "Is exegesis really a theological activity, or can it become one?" (p. 11). Barr's question is odd. For example, we could substitute an activity for "exegesis" and ask the same question: is the critical study of texts, in their original languages, really a theological activity, or can it become one? What if the text is in Latin and its author is St. Thomas Aquinas? What if it is in German and its author is Martin Luther? Or, what if it is the Greek text of Chalcedon? Can the critical study of St. Thomas or Luther or Chalcedon really be or become a theological activity? Of course it can, I suppose everyone would agree. We could test the supposition by checking to see what theologians do when they are theologically active; some of them study the texts of St. Thomas, or of Martin Luther, or—more rarely—of Chalcedon. Some of them, as it still happens, also do critical study of biblical texts. But Barr knows that his question is odd, and so he puts the question more "realistically" (his term): as theologians—Barr says dogmaticians—how do we allow our theology, or our "dogmatic principles" to be "influenced, enriched or modified by the impact of actual biblical material?" (p. 13).

This more realistic form of the question, as Barr takes it to be, covers some assumptions that ought to be exposed. By "dogmatic principles" Barr seems to mean those basic elements of Christian faith that we inherit, if we are Christians, almost natively. And by "actual biblical material" Barr seems to mean the conception of the Bible we would acquire if we were theological students in one of Oxford's colleges. In saying that such students do not, at least as a rule, learn to do exegesis from James Barr and then, on that basis, form a set of dogmatic principles—but rather, they come to the study of biblical exegesis as committed believers, and for that reason—Barr is surely correct. And that is the basis for his realistic question: why does the biblical exegesis theological students learn to do at Oxford have no reforming impact on their dogmatic principles? Of this more realistic question Barr asks another: "why has it not generally been expressed in this way?" (p. 13). In other words, why have we first defined the practice of exegesis and then asked whether or how this practice can become theological, rather than beginning with theology and asking how exegesis fits within it?

In attempting to answer this question, Barr seems to get sidetracked. In fact, he takes the question to be asking something slightly different: why do theologians—or theological students, in his example—fail to revise their theological convictions when the Bible undermines them? That leads him into a discussion of presuppositions, theological or religious ones, and he lands yet another fatal blow against the notion that documents of faith can be *understood* only from within these presuppositions or convictions. So stated, the notion is false; there is no harm in pointing that out once more, but it is a diversion from Barr's argument. Barr gets on track again by pointing out that, theologically

considered, "in exegesis Scripture is set over against existing theological belief: not as an antagonist, indeed, but in the hope and expectation of fruitful
interaction" (p. 17).

This last point seems unassailable and in accord with the history of
biblical theology adumbrated above, in section II. But Barr himself has here
moved away from the question that opens his essay. That question asks about
exegesis as a theological *activity*, while Barr has gone on to talk about the
Bible and "dogmatic principles," about two different but putatively interrelated *texts*, if you will.[32] The difference between an activity and a text is not
trivial. Without incorporating them within some activity, some kind of reading,
it is hard to think how texts could be interrelated. The two "texts," Scripture
and dogmatics, have been interrelated in a wide variety of ways, each of them
incorporating Scripture in a different kind of activity. The Bible could be the
type of which dogmatics is the antitype. Sometimes, texts have been
interrelated in that way. The Bible could be a set of allegories, the literal
sense of which theology sets out; a collection of metaphors that theology uses
to redescribe reality; a comprehensive but unharmonious manual of doctrine
that theology puts in harmonious, coherent, and contemporary form; a set of
historical facts whose significance theology extrapolates; a literary expression
of religious experience that theology seeks to reoccasion in contemporary
readers. All of these are ways of relating texts to each other, and are thus
ways of conceiving the activity or practice of theology. What is more, the Bible
itself cannot rule against, or for, any of them. The Bible cannot, that is, simply
set *itself* "over against existing theological belief."

That is so because texts cannot tell us what we must do with them. The
Bible contains a good bit of instruction, for example, but it cannot tell us to
treat its instructions or laws *as* laws—or as halakah—to guide our behavior or
to shape our communities. We can use the Bible's laws as historical or
anthropological evidence, rather than as moral and cultic instruction. We can
study biblical law as a literary genre, or as sociological data, or as any
number of other things; our decisions to do so are our own, not the Bible's.
Gibbon's history of Rome's decline and fall is sometimes cited as an example
of the same thing: it is written as a history but is frequently, perhaps usually,
studied as a literary text. Gibbon's text is now, perhaps, more easily
incorporated within the activity of literary criticism than within that of historical research on the Roman empire. Psychologists may be more interested than
theologians, or Christians practicing the devotional life, in St. Augustine's
Confessions. Similarly, we determine how we will use the Bible according to
the activity in which we are engaged—not according to any law internal to the
text itself, but in accordance with some more or less rule-governed practice.
One such practice is theology—we can say that much without deciding what
theology is.

A statement of "theological beliefs," as Barr calls them, will often
include some account of theology's own practice. Furthermore, theology will

either assume as part of its practice, or state as a component of its beliefs, some particular way in which Scripture is to be used. In some cases, a chapter on hermeneutics is the first chapter of a systematic theology; it is so in the Dogmatics of David Friedrich Strauss and, according to Eberhard Jüngel, of Karl Barth.[33] Such chapters are not only, and sometimes not at all, a summary of customary academic practice in the interpretation of texts; rather, they are much more like a policy statement: "In my theological activity, and for these reasons, this is the use I shall make of the Bible." The policy differs, of course, according to what one takes theology to be.[34]

This, too, Barr understands: "theological consequence does not follow directly from the text itself but only from its interaction with other texts and with pre-existing theological tradition" ("Exegesis," p 23). He does not entirely approve of it, however. In a lengthy discussion of the "Quest of the historical Jesus" (p. 24), Barr criticizes Martin Kähler for opposing that quest on theological grounds. His specific criticism is, on this point, that Kähler's "whole argument is predicated entirely upon one particular type of Christianity, his own, and does not consider how the question might work from within a different total structure of theology." (p. 37). Whatever Barr means by a "total structure of theology"—perhaps a comprehensively systematic theology—he links it with Kähler's "particular type of Christianity." Kähler's particular type of Christianity is then commensurate with, presumably, a particular systematic theology, which includes a set of remarks on its relation to Scripture. That particular relation, in turn, is such that "nothing relevant to Christian faith can be gained by going behind the testimony as we have it in the Bible" (p. 37)—Barr's summary of Kähler's remarks. But Barr objects to this coordination among a particular type of Christianity, a particular systematic theology commensurate with it, and an equally particular view of this theology's relation to Scripture. His objection seems to center on Kähler's refusal to consider "all the possibilities"—including, perhaps, the possibility that something theologically constructive (or usefully deconstructive) might be learned from research on the historical Jesus. And this refusal, Barr says, "is symptomatic." It is symptomatic, specifically, of the motivation among theologians "to find a satisfactory position for the question of the historical Jesus within their own theological system." These theological positions "were never worked out on the basis of what happened in practical interpretative work" (p. 37).

These latter comments of Barr's are somewhat obscure.[35] Barr could mean (a) that theologians like Kähler failed to ground their remarks about the historical Jesus in the results of historical inquiry. If that were the case, they would fail as a criticism. There is no general rule requiring systematic theology, whether ordered to a particular Christian confession or not, to ground its remarks about Jesus exclusively in the results of historical inquiry.[36] Or, Barr could mean (b) that theologians like Kähler were mistaken about what historical inquiry is actually in a position to determine about Jesus. This is a potentially pertinent criticism, depending on whether such mistakes were and are, in fact, made. Finally, Barr could mean (c) that it is theologically mistaken to dismiss research into the historical Jesus. Perhaps Barr means a combination of these last two: theologians like Kähler were and are mistaken both about what historical inquiry can achieve with respect to Jesus, and mistaken as well about the theological importance of this kind of inquiry. Barr says quite explicitly that "belief in the Christ of the apostolic witness must necessarily imply some adequate continuity with what he did, and thought, and said, and was, in his earthly ministry" ("Exegesis," p. 35), and this necessary implication of Christian belief warrants attention to historical inquiry.

It is not crucial here to decide between Barr and Kähler. Of importance to our discussion is that the issue between them, as Barr casts it, is an explicitly theological one. The quest of the historical Jesus does not assume importance only because historians can pursue such a quest, and pursue it legitimately; it becomes important for the explicitly theological reason Barr cites—it is a *necessary implication* of Christian belief, as Barr (and surely not only James Barr) construes Christian belief. "Theological beliefs," for Barr no less than for Kähler, include an at least implicit account of theology's practice. And theological practice includes, for both, a particular way—perhaps a particular variety of ways—in which Scripture is to be used. That use is not simply *determined* by narrowly theological considerations alone. Barr and Kähler make their arguments in conversation with, or in response to, historical inquiry as actually practiced, and the conclusions it actually reaches, in their quite different respective contexts. In spite of that qualification's importance, however,[37] the judgments of both Kähler and Barr about the historical interpretation of Scripture are explicitly theological. They concern the appropriate relation of Scripture to theology.

I V
Biblical Theology and Christian Confession

In another essay, "The Theological Case Against Biblical Theology," Barr claims that, in the biblical theology movement, "nothing was more vehemently opposed than the idea that the biblical scholar should be primarily a historian."[38] The claim is striking. If we may take as canonical Brevard Childs's description of that movement, then it included H. H. Rowley and G. Ernest Wright among its spokesmen. As biblical scholars, and by virtue of their education and their research, both were primarily historians, and no one insisted more vigorously than did G. Ernest Wright on the theological importance of historical research.[39] There may be room for argument whether the work of Wright is not, in fact, primarily theological rather than historical, but that argument should not beg its central question. To claim, as Barr does, that according to the biblical theologians, "it was quite wrong to suppose that historical research into the Bible could lead to wholesome theological results," ("The Theological Case," p. 5) does beg the question. It does so unless we should concede that research assuming the contrary is, by definition, not historical. In fact, the biblical theologians were concerned not merely to inject historical research with a theological purpose, but also to sponsor or support a particular notion of theology itself—one that would have their kind of historical research at the heart of its interests. I believe they would have agreed with the statement, just contrary to Barr's own assessment of them, that biblical scholars should be primarily historians (in their view, what else?), *if* their scholarship is to be theologically interesting. Apart from such a statement, it is impossible to understand them *as biblical theologians*, given the very predominantly and intentionally historical character of their work.[40]

Only in this light can we agree with Barr's further observation, that there were "basic theological reasons against the claims of biblical theology" ("The Theological Case," p. 6). The eventual demise of biblical theology, Barr claims, was brought about, not by its own internal problems, but by the hostility toward it of "theology, as theology" (p. 6). I take Barr here to be speaking of theologians—those engaged in "theology, as theology"—who were not biblical scholars and who had, in addition, their own theological reasons for opposing the biblical theology movement and perhaps anything that would call itself biblical theology. In other words, there were theologies and theologians for whom the work of *biblical* theologians was simply not pertinent, and who rejected or had important disagreements with the kind of theology to which these biblical scholars and biblical theologians could make a material contribution. Unfortunately, Barr does not go on to make his case, saying only that "nowhere, perhaps, were these [basic theological reasons against the claims of biblical theology] expressly stated, and to this extent we have to imagine for ourselves what was in people's minds" (p. 6). We do not need to rely on our imagination in order to appreciate the plausibility of his suggestion: biblical theology was compatible with only some kinds, and not with others, of what Barr calls "real theology" (p. 10). Whatever its internal problems may have been, and however much they may have contributed to its decline, the biblical theology movement Barr describes and criticizes had a substantial part of its rationale in a more or less specific kind of "theology, as theology."

Barr himself draws attention to this, observing that some theologians "felt that biblical theology was a partisan movement" (p. 8). Indeed it was, but its partisan character cannot be understood only as an academic affinity for neo-orthodox theology or for Karl Barth, as Barr proposes. The biblical theologians themselves were often very critical of Barth, particularly of his views on history and historical criticism, but on other matters as well.[41] Academic factors were not alone decisive in the emergence of biblical theology. Childs points to some of the other factors in his account of the movement; for example, he notes that "the most aggressive leaders in the new movement were often

Presbyterian in background or affiliation . . . ," and that throughout, "the real impetus of the movement continued to center in the Free Church wing of Protestantism. . . ."[42] Childs attributes this heavy Presbyterian participation to the fundamentalist-modernist controversy through which that group had come, and to which biblical theology held out hope of being a solution. But it is also appropriate to ask why this group would favor an approach to—or a use of—the Bible that promised to solve this particular controversy, and even why they would think it important. One answer to these questions is surely to be found in the churchly identity of those whom Childs places in the leadership of the biblical theology movement. By vocation, as seminary or divinity school teachers, *and* by confession, they were committed to an integral and credible relation between Scripture and theology. They did not come to this commitment as the result of philosophical and theological developments on the continent, however much those developments may have helped them, or emboldened them, to articulate it. G. Ernest Wright, as an example, did not require Emil Brunner—leave alone Karl Barth—to tell him, as one at home in and committed to the Reformed tradition, that Scripture and theology have to be related. His partisan stance on this issue was unrelated to any specifically Barthian sympathies—Wright seems to have had none—and the issue could not be resolved, credibly, by either of the choices offered by fundamentalism and modernism.

In his essay, "Wanted: A Biblical Theology," in the inaugural issue of *Theology Today*, Paul Minear attacked the cleavage between "Biblical historians" and theologians perpetuated in seminary departments of Bible and theology, and complained that "in graduate schools which train Bible teachers, the Ph.D. program requires no grounding in *confessional* theology."[43] And Childs, too, mentions the importance to biblical theology of the possibility that biblical criticism could be used "without reservation as a valid tool while at the same time recovering a robust, *confessionally* oriented theology."[44] This emphasis on the confessional character of theology may seem striking and even out of place as a concern of biblical scholars, and it lies behind Barr's characterization of biblical theology as "a partisan movement." It was so, Barr claims, because biblical theologians "lined up on one side of a series of disagreements that were really a matter for doctrinal theologians to discuss among themselves" ("The Theological Case," p. 8). While we can appreciate the whimsy of Barr's image of "doctrinal theologians" convening privately to decide whether, for example, the Bible is "authoritative in a degree not comparable with any other human cultural manifestation" (p. 7), it also helps diagnose the problem. For whom should the doctrinal magesterium decide this question, and on what grounds?[45]

Barr is quite right: by itself, biblical theology cannot determine whether or how theology will relate itself to the Bible ("The Theological Case," pp. 10-11). On what basis, though, can "doctrinal theologians," or does "real theology" (p. 10), presume to make this determination? According to Barr, biblical theologians are unable to resolve these issues, not because they lack competence—he says that most have studied doctrinal theology—but because "they do not dispose of material that will enable them to judge and decide the question;" (p. 10) "they do not have the *material* to which they can turn" (p. 11, emphasis his). Here Barr acknowledges what we claimed above, that the Bible cannot determine how it will be used or to what end: texts cannot tell us what we must do with them. In Barr's own words, "Any decision about what is or is not theology depends on going outside the circle of directly *biblical* guidance" (p. 11, emphasis his). As noted in the preceding paragraph, Barr relies on doctrinal theologians to settle the question: ". . . it must be a question of entirely open discussion in the general realm of doctrinal and philosophical theology" (p. 11). I believe we should welcome such open discussions, even though I cannot see any way that philosophical theology could resolve the question at issue—"it does not dispose of" the relevant material. But neither do I see why biblical theologians are at any disadvantage in such a discussion. Barr is himself eloquent and living testimony that biblical scholars can dispose of material beyond that of the Bible. If they can dispose, as Barr does, of the material of linguistics, or as others do, of sociological, literary, and historical theory, then doctrinal and philosophical theology should be well within their grasp; its material is no less accessible.[46] Biblical scholars have never been content to rely on "directly *biblical* guidance" in pursuing any inquiry. How could they be? Why should they be content do do so with theology? But more than that—how does the material specific to doctrinal and philosophical theology put those who dispose of it in a position to resolve the question of theology's relation to Scripture?

The concerns of Minear and Childs may be illuminating. Following his analysis of biblical theology's crisis, Childs asks why biblical theology, of a more disciplined sort, will continue to be required. One important reason is practical: "Christian pastors continue to do their own Biblical Theology," and they do so *as Christian pastors*—"By the very nature" of their office. On this accounting, should Barr's conventicle of doctrinal theologians declare all biblical theology irrelevant, their declaration would be correspondingly irrelevant to the work of those Christian pastors for whom Scripture's role is given in the nature of their office.[47] For these Christian pastors, if for no one else, Scripture's importance to theology is a confessional, a vocational, and thus a practical matter. On this accounting, biblical theology will assume a decidedly partisan stance in favor of the kind of theology that regards "biblical teaching" to be "the basis of our talk about God."[48] That these terms are Karl Barth's does not mean that biblical theology is necessarily biased in favor of Barthian, or of what has come to be called neo-orthodox theology; it means only that Barth took 'Dogmatics' to be "the self-examination [*Selbstprüfung*] of the Christian Church in respect of the content of its distinctive talk about God,"[49] and that this corresponds to—or it is compatible with—the confession, vocation, and practice of at least some Christian pastors. The bias is entirely on the part of Barth, and it is a bias grounded in what he and at least some Christian pastors take the Christian church and its talk of God to be.[50]

V
Constructing a Relation

In the two preceding sections of this essay I have argued—with the help of James Barr—that the problems biblical theology has inherited are theological in nature. They concern primarily the appropriate relation of Scripture to theology, and, partly as a consequence, the relation of biblical to systematic or doctrinal theology. I have also argued that biblical theologians should—as Barr himself does—make theological judgments about these problems, and cannot avoid doing so if they want to be clear about the nature and purpose of their work.

Throughout, I have maintained that how we understand the *relation* of biblical to systematic theology depends, in turn, on how we understand each of these. I have also tried to show that, in the course of its history, biblical theology has tended to emerge, in different forms, when a question has been raised about the appropriateness of some theology's relation to Scripture. The point of calling it 'biblical' theology has often been, then, a critical and polemical one. That point has depended on the conviction or the confession that, in its function as Scripture, the Bible is foundational, as we may say, to Christian communities, and hence to any explication of Christian faith.[51] Christian communities may come to a differing conviction; if they do, I cannot see that biblical theology on any definition has warrants specific to itself for showing them to be wrong. It cannot be the task of biblical theology, then, to make a case for the foundational importance of Scripture to Christian communities. On this account, and in the argument of this essay, biblical theology depends on such foundational importance, and thus on the identity and practice of at least some Christian communities.[52]

A. *Scripture as Foundational*
These claims require some clarification. In what sense can Scripture be foundational to Christian communities? As I understand the matter, the Bible as Scripture is foundational to Christian communities if it is indispensable to their identity, and if its use is integral to their practice, *as Christian* communities.[53] And it is just in this sense, I am proposing, that biblical theology depends on the identity and practice of Christian communities, namely, those for whom Scripture is foundational. The way in which different communities have their identity, indispensably, in relation to Scripture can vary; the variety will matter to biblical theology but does not undermine it. And even within Christian communities, or among those who share a common

way of having their identity in relation to Scripture, the uses of Scripture will also vary. As David Kelsey observes, "scripture is used in a wide variety of activities that constitute the common life of Christian communities: in liturgy, preaching, education, counsel, controversy, even governance."[54] Scripture will still be foundational to these communities—apart from it, on their own self-definition, they would not be *Christian* communities—but there is no one, uniform use of Scripture that all of these activities have in common.

If for some Christian communities Scripture is foundational—that is, indispensable to their identity, and its use integral to their practice—and if systematic theology is one of the activities in which Christian communities engage, perhaps in dependence on others, then it seems to follow that Scripture is foundational to systematic theology. And if *that* makes sense, then it may also seem that we have solved the formal problem this essay addresses: biblical theology lays the foundation on which systematic theology builds. While this is one view of their relation, and a traditional one—it was Gabler's view, for example[55]—the earlier parts of this essay, and especially our conversation with James Barr, have at least pointed to some respects in which it is unsatisfactory. Even if Scripture is foundational to systematic theology, it does not follow that biblical theology is. Here it is appropriate to recall the distinction I drew earlier (section III) between texts and practices. As a text, the Bible is foundational, on some definitions, to the practice of systematic theology, and that the Bible is in some sense foundational to biblical theology seems self-evident. However, it does not follow from any of this that one practice (biblical theology) is foundational to the other (systematic theology).

I propose that the relation between biblical and systematic theology is more complex and at least potentially more fruitful than the traditional view represents. Such a proposal requires, minimally, that we have a definition of theology that makes sense of the identity and practice of Christian communities, and can take into account Scripture's foundational character in those communities. Hans Frei has offered a definition that seems to fit these requirements:

> One could say that theology is part of the heritable social currency of a specific religious community, the Christian church. It is its self-critical inquiry into the use of its language for purposes of applying and handing it on for use by the same developing and changing community in the future. It presupposes connection to another, more elemental use of the same communal language, that is, the constant transition from the Christian religious affections to their kerygmatic, rhetorical, and finally their descriptively didactic linguistic shape.[56]

This definition, which is Frei's paraphrase of Friedrich Schleiermacher, accords with what I have said is an activity in which Christian communities engage. They do so, it is sufficient here to say, for reasons internal to themselves and consistent with their identity. It ought to be clear, since Frei is describing Schleiermacher, that this definition of theology does not conceive biblical theology as foundational to systematic theology. When Schleiermacher does speak of biblical theology—in his terms, "exegetical theology" or "scriptural dogmatics"—he conceives of it as complementary or coordinate, but not foundational, to systematic theology or *Glaubenslehre*.[57] Scripture is nonetheless foundational to systematic theology, on Schleiermacher's account, but not *directly* foundational. That is, systematic theology is grounded directly in the church's confessional documents, which is to say, in the Symbols of the Evangelical Church, and specifically, the Prussian union of the Lutheran and Reformed churches. But given the character and confession of that church, Scripture (but only the New Testament) is *indirectly* basic to systematic theology as Schleiermacher conceives it and carries it out. Schleiermacher makes this point explicitly:

> Thus the direct appeal to Scripture is only necessary either when the use which the confessional documents make of the New Testament books cannot be approved of (and we must at least admit the possibility that in individual cases all the testimonies adduced, even if not falsely applied, may nevertheless be unsatisfying, since other passages of Scripture must be applied as means of proof), or when propositions of the confessional documents do not themselves seem sufficiently scriptural or Protestant, and these must accordingly be superannuated and other expressions substituted, which will then certainly the more easily find acceptance, the more it is shown that Scripture on the whole favours them or even perhaps demands them.[58]

It may be that systematic theology's appeal to Scripture will need to be more constant, if it is to be in a position to assess, at every point along the way, the confessional documents' use of it. And by the same token, there will likely need to be some available sense of "Scripture on the whole." It is sometimes considered biblical theology's task to determine the sense of "Scripture on the whole," a sense that systematic theology could then use in its own and distinctive task. This solution seems premature, however, and not only because biblical theologians have been perennially unsuccessful in achieving it. Perhaps the Bible is not susceptible of the kind of wholeness (or unity) biblical theologians have traditionally sought, or perhaps biblical theology as usually conceived is not equipped to make sense of Scripture on the whole.[59] In any event, Schleiermacher is talking about systematic rather than biblical theology, and precisely about systematic theology's critical appeal to Scripture in describing the "collective consciousness" of a specific Christian community.[60] The sources for that description are the confessional documents, but they are occasionally inadequate relative to Scripture. In that case, direct appeal to Scripture is warranted and necessary in support of "other

sions"—other than those in the confessions. And their conformity with "Scripture on the whole" will win acceptance for these expressions, since they will thus show themselves to be more adequate expressions (precisely) of the collective consciousness of the specific Christian community in question.

I believe there is a strong compatibility in Schleiermacher's view between the collective consciousness of a Christian community and a determinate sense of Scripture on the whole. That is what I propose here—namely, that a Christian community is itself a kind of commentary on Scripture, as an embodied and enacted construal of "Scripture on the whole." In other words, the life and character of a Christian community is a proposal about Scripture's wholeness. And if that is the case, then Frei's remark about theology as that kind of community's "self-critical inquiry into the use of its language" creates a space and a rationale for biblical theology's relation to systematic theology.

B. *Biblical Theology's Systematic Framework*

Even if we have succeeded, with the help of Frei and Schleiermacher, in creating a space in which to relate biblical and systematic theology, we have not yet defined biblical theology's rationale. Its relation to systematic theology is biblical theology's primary rationale. Rather, its primary rationale is the use of Scripture in relation to those activities or practices that "constitute the common life of Christian communities."[61] In other words, (1) there is a use of Christian communal language "more elemental" than theology's own use of it. Furthermore, (2) just as the Christian religious affections acquire (or simply *have*) a kerygmatic or rhetorical but inevitably "linguistic shape," so the practices constitutive of Christian communities are themselves predominantly linguistic—kerygmatic, rhetorical, and even discursive. Finally, (3) the Christian religious affections have their specific linguistic shape, and constitutive Christian practices have their linguistic character, in self-conscious relation to Scripture. If this is the case—or I should say, *when* this is the case—then the interpretation of Scripture is intrinsic to Christian identity. It is intrinsic not only in the sense that a Christian community must engage in explicit and specific acts of interpretation in order to maintain its identity; it is also intrinsic in the more elemental sense I have suggested, in dependence on Frei (and Schleiermacher). That is, a specific religious community's affections and practices represent a kind of commentary on Scripture and a construal of Scripture on the whole; they represent judgments, even if merely *ad hoc* or implicit, about Scripture's wholeness and its significant patterns.[62]

Biblical theology has its rationale in just this character of at least some Christian communities. Such a linguistic or even rhetorical community[63] has a strong natural interest in assessing the appropriateness of the more elemental use of its language (in other words, its first-order language), and hence the appropriateness of its kerygmatic, rhetorical, and discursive practices. Given what was said in the preceding paragraph, this will necessarily include an assessment of such a community's use of Scripture, and thus of its explicit and implicit interpretation.[64]   Or, to use Schleiermacher's language, this will include an assessment whether the religious affections of a given Christian community are genuinely Christian. *In so far as* such a community claims (minimally) that its affections are shaped in relation to Scripture—and thus constitutes, as I would say, an implicit commentary on Scripture and a specific but variable construal of Scripture's wholeness—such assessment makes a legitimate and necessary appeal to Scripture.   It is the proposal of this essay that such assessment is the defining task of biblical theology.

C. Biblical Theology and Normative Discourse

An immediate implication of this proposal, a proposal that lacks any uniqueness whatever, is that biblical theology is one dimension of a Christian community's "self-critical inquiry into the use of its language."[65] And an immediate implication of *that* claim is that biblical theology presupposes—it does not invent—a set of linguistic practices, ranging from kerygmatic to discursive. And included among those discursive practices is systematic theology. If systematic theology is a Christian community's critical self-description, and if for such a community Scripture is foundational, then systematic theology will both presuppose and articulate a communal practice of self-assessment in relation to Scripture.   In the case of both biblical and systematic theology, a given community is basic.[66]   A Christian community, then, will include implicit or explicit rules for communal self-assessment; in Schleiermacher's case, the communal rules were represented principally by the Evangelical confessions. These communal rules did not, for Schleiermacher, eliminate all direct appeals to Scripture. They did, however, provide a normative framework for determining the kinds of appeal to Scripture that would count.   To put it differently, the church of the Prussian union constituted a community of interest—a community whose precise interests in Scripture, as confessionally defined, set the terms according to which appeals to Scripture could be included in "normative discourse."

I have borrowed the latter term from Jeffrey Stout, who says, regarding ethics, that

> by presupposing standards not currently in doubt among
> members of my community, I am using or relying on those
> standards in a way that commits me to their authority. This
> is what places me within the logical space of normative
> discourse, the only space in which expressions like "is justi-
> fied" and "is true" can be used, not merely mentioned.[67]

Schleiermacher occupies the logical space of normative discourse by using standards in a way that commits him to their authority.   The principal standards he uses are the Evangelical confessions, on the basis of which he can assess certain samples of Christian speech as true, and certain proposals about

Christian speech as justified. When Schleiermacher says of his pronouncements on the divine act of justification, "But the truth is this," he is using "is
true" and not merely mentioning it.[68] Schleiermacher's use of standards not
then in doubt among members of his community did not commit him to agree
with everything his community said or believed, nor did it commit him simply
to accept those standards uncritically; it committed him to their authority as
situated expressions of the community whose faith he was describing—and, as
it happens, redescribing. Schleiermacher knew his systematic theology was
occasional, as was the community for which we wrote it. In any event, a given
community remained basic.[69]

   If biblical theology participates, as I am arguing, in a Christian community's self-assessment, then it will have to attend to the terms in which that
assessment is carried out, and to rules governing the use of those terms. For
biblical no less than for systematic theology, then, a community is basic; more
specifically, a given linguistic and rhetorical community is basic—a community
that not only has a particular language but is especially interested in the
appropriate use of that language. It is only within what Stout calls "the logical space of normative discourse" that biblical theology *can* participate in a
community's self-assessment. If for the Christian community this assessment
consists in a self-critical inquiry into the use of its language, then biblical
theology has to take account of—indeed, it has to presuppose—the kerygmatic,
rhetorical, and discursive uses of that language. *These* uses of *this* language
form the standards that biblical theology presupposes, if it stands in the
logical space of normative theological discourse. But is not that logical space
occupied precisely by systematic theology? While systematic theology stands
in that space, it does not fully occupy it. In fact, systematic theology (on the
definition given above) is the paradigm instance of Christian discursive practice.[70] But if this is the case, and I think it is so self-evidently, then the relation
between biblical and systematic theology is quite different from, if not just the
reverse of, the traditional view I noted earlier in this section, that biblical
theology lays the foundation on which systematic theology builds. To the
contrary, I am proposing, systematic theology is an indispensable framework
of biblical theology.[71]

D. Biblical Theology's Descriptive Vocabulary

   A framework is different from a foundation, and the change in metaphor
is significant. Foundational to both systematic and biblical theology is a set of
communal practices, whose rules for self-assessment systematic theology both
presupposes and articulates.   It may also propose revisions; but as
Schleiermacher says, these "seldom proceed directly from the dogmatic discussions themselves, but are for the most part occasioned, in one way or
another, by the proceedings of public worship or by popular literature for the
dissemination of religion."[72]   This, too, emphasizes the governing point: a

community is basic. It is in systematic theology's articulation of the community's rules or standards for self-assessment, and in its use of both those standards and the community's language itself, that biblical theology has systematic theology as its framework. And that framework serves precisely to define the logical space of normative discourse, and to provide for biblical theology a descriptive vocabulary.[73] The latter point is crucial because of what I observed earlier: texts do not tell us what to do with them, or how we should relate them to other texts. Nor is it sufficient to say of biblical theology that it is descriptive—that it *describes* biblical texts or some features of their content. Such a statement is true but trivially so, since virtually all the interesting and contested issues concern what we are to describe and in what terms. Those issues are implicit in virtually every proposal in biblical theology's history (they *are* biblical theology's history, one might say).

In her treatment of metaphor, Janet Martin Soskice argues for the importance of an interpretive tradition linked with Saul Kripke's notion of a linguistic community.[74] Any speaker, says Soskice, is a member of a particular linguistic community; further:

> The descriptive vocabulary which any individual uses is, in turn, dependent on the community of interest and investigation in which he finds himself, and the descriptive vocabulary which a community has at its disposal is embedded in particular traditions of investigation and conviction.[75]
>
> . . . .
>
> Corresponding to the scientific communities of interest, there are religious communities of interest (Christians, for example) which are bound by shared assumptions, interest, and traditions of interpretation, and share a descriptive vocabulary.[76]

A Christian community provides biblical theology its descriptive vocabulary, embedded in particular traditions of investigation and conviction—and in a particular set of linguistic practices. One of those practices, systematic theology, is discursive. In so far as biblical theology participates in such a community's self-assessment—or its self-critical inquiry into the use of its language—it has systematic theology as its framework. Biblical theology is not "theological" because it uncovers "a 'theological' stratum of an ancient literature" (Farley), or because "the contents of the Bible are of decisive significance for Christian teaching and practice."[77] It is theological—this is my proposal—because it shares with systematic theology, as a Christian community's discursive practice, the logical space of normative discourse. This explains, I think, why Minear and Childs had the temerity to suggest that biblical theology has something to do with confessional theology.[78]

That biblical theology is a descriptive activity is a virtual commonplace. However, it is insufficiently recognized that an interpreter (or a community of interpreters) necessarily chooses the terms, the vocabulary, of any description.[79] In the case of Scripture, terms at home in Christian linguistic practice often find their way into biblical interpretation, but they are more mentioned than used. For example, John Barton has recently suggested that critical reconstructions of Israel's history raised, or should have raised, "enormous questions about how the history thus reconstructed could be seen as providentially guided."[80] "Providence" is obviously a piece of Christian theological vocabulary, and to show why or how Christian theologians need to revise their notion of God's providence Barton would need first to consider how that term is used in at least some samples of Christian discursive practice. It could turn out that a reconstruction of Israel's history does indeed call for revisions in Christian talk of providence, but to show this would require using "providence" as part of a descriptive vocabulary applied to the study of Scripture. James Barr suggests precisely the same thing, in respect of at least some Christian kerygmatic practice, when he claims that "belief in the Christ of apostolic witness must necessarily imply some adequate continuity with what he did, and thought, and said, and was, in his earthly ministry."[81] His criticism of various biblical scholars and theologians is determined in part by what he regards as their failure to take into account what Christian believers mean when they express faith in the apostolic witness. His disagreement is within the logical space of normative discourse, and specifically within Christian discursive practice, and his recommendation is embedded within a particular tradition of conviction. To carry forward either investigation, Barton's or Barr's, would be to commit an act of biblical theology.

VI
Conclusion

The proposal I have developed seems (1) just the reverse of what biblical theology has been at crucial points in its history—a critical response to systematic theology, and specifically to systematic theology's relation to Scripture. Moreover, it seems (2) to erase the clear distinction between biblical and systematic (or dogmatic) theology that Gabler advocated, and on which biblical theology has sometimes insisted, and to collapse the two disciplines or activities into one. Finally, it seems (3) to rob biblical theology of its critical and revisionary potential by subordinating it to the actual practice of particular communities—or of a particular community. That it merely *seems* to fail in these ways suggests that I do not regard it to have done so. I will address these apparent failings individually, in this conclusion.

(1) Biblical theology as a critical response to systematic theology has depended on a judgment that some systematic theology's relation to Scripture is inappropriate. The grounds for such a judgment have varied (see section I, above). In some cases, such a judgment has depended on religious grounds,

and thus on some version of a community's first-order use of Scripture—its use in kerygmatic and rhetorical practice. In these cases, biblical theology's argument has amounted to a systematic theological one—an argument, for example, that systematic theology has vacated the logical space of normative discourse. Gabler's original proposal for biblical theology was just such a judgment: it was a systematic theological judgment that dogmatic theology (in his case) had endangered its foundation in truth. My proposal does not assume that all systematic theology is always in that situation. It depends on a definition of theology drawn from Frei, who drew it from Schleiermacher. In relation to other definitions of systematic theology, the proposal would look quite different.

(2) I have no worry that biblical theology is in danger of collapsing into systematic theology. At the same time, a distinction between them is not essential. Gabler's argument for such a distinction depended on philosophy's ability to show what in Scripture is historical and thus dispensable; dogmatics takes from Scripture only what philosophy can show is not merely historical but true.[82] Philosophy having given up its truth-legislating powers over history, we are no longer bound by the distinction Gabler invented. But while it is not essential, a division of linguistic labor (Hilary Putnam's phrase) between biblical and systematic theology is useful. Biblical theology concerns itself specifically with what Stout calls normative and explanatory accounts— accounts of Scripture, in our case—and with negotiating the differences.[83] Explanatory and normative accounts are not the same thing. We may want an account of, say, John's Gospel to explain its redaction, its differences from the synoptics, and its social location. But we also want an account of John's Gospel as a witness to Jesus Christ. We are likely to prefer accounts that hold these two aims together as nearly as possible, and there is nothing odd about that preference. As Stout says,

> It is anything but unusual...for normative and explanatory
> aims to work in tandem, each informing and constraining the
> other in the labor of interpretation. The normative aims you
> hold will influence the explanations you seek. The shape
> your explanations take will in part determine the normative
> aims you can reasonably pursue.[84]

Normative aims are shaped in relation to what Soskice calls a community of interest and investigation, and what Stout calls "the interests, purposes, and background beliefs of interpreters." Explanatory accounts sometimes contribute to reshaping those aims, interests, purposes, and beliefs—and even those communities. That is a prudential and theological justification for a division of labor. Nonetheless, biblical theologians can in principle reflect competently on normative aims, and systematic theologians—or philosophical ones—can in principle offer competent explanatory accounts. Nothing positive accrues to biblical theology, or to anything important, by insisting on its complete independence. The danger is greater when biblical theologians, or systematic ones, defer entirely to each other.

(3) For some of the reasons just given, biblical theology (on my proposal) is not inherently conservative. Biblical theology depends on the linguistic practices of Christian communities, but it also depends on the interests those communities have in assessing the appropriateness of their practices in relation to Scripture. My proposal does not assume any one criterion of appropriateness, nor does it assume any one, specific pattern for relating a community's practice to Scripture. It does assume that Scripture can function critically in relation to any of the linguistic practices—kerygmatic, rhetorical, or discursive. Kathryn Tanner makes a similar point by distinguishing between the text and its plain sense, on the one and, and interpretation on the other. Any exposition of the text, she says, including any proffered account of its plain sense, is itself an interpretation and thus *distinct from* the text and its plain sense. In short, the plain sense of the text is

> unavailable in any form distinct from the text itself. The plain sense of the text becomes an independently unspecifiable locus of meaning, something that transcends any and all attempts to reformulate it. As such it functions critically even with respect to consensus readings of a text; it works to evacuate the pretentions of communal discourse generally.[85]

Since, on Tanner's accounting, it is always *we* who specify Scripture's plain sense, and since the text perdures through any specifications of its plain sense, Scripture remains a potential focus of and for self-criticism. Biblical theology is not the only way such self-criticism and reform can come about, but neither is it bound to stand in the way by celebrating the pretentions of communal discourse. Christian communities are rhetorical, not deductive.

The relation between biblical and systematic theology I have proposed, or constructed, is meant as a response to the needs of Christian communities. It does not have its starting point or rationale in the demands and possibilities of an academic discipline.[86] Neither do I think it ignores either the demands or the possibilities. But the question is not just whether biblical theology can or ought to do what I have here proposed for it in relation to systematic theology; the question is also how some Christian communities should conduct their necessary self-critical inquiry in relation to Scripture. If biblical theologians tend strictly to other things, biblical theology will probably go on, or emerge, in their place. To rephrase Etienne Gilson's remark, biblical theology always buries its undertakers.[87]

Notes

1   M. H. Goshen-Gottstein, "Tanakh Theology: The Religion of the Old Testament and the Place of Jewish Biblical Theology," in *Ancient Israelite Religion*, ed. P. D. Miller, Jr., P. D. Hanson, S. D. McBride (Philadelphia: Fortress, 1987), 626.

2   It is not obvious that biblical theology is, technically, a discipline. For a discussion of what constitutes a discipline, see Stephen Toulmin, *Human Understanding* (Princeton: Princeton University Press, 1972); Edward Farley, *The Fragility of Knowledge* (Philadelphia: Fortress Press, 1988), 29-55, 109. Biblical and systematic theology could be considered speciality areas within the discipline of theology. Matters seem particularly complicated for Old Testament theology, if it wants to be both a historical and a theological discipline. See M. H. Goshen-Gottstein, "Tanakh Theology," 614-44; W. H. Schmidt, "Die Frage nach der Einheit des Alten Testaments—im Spannungsfeld von Religionsgeschichte und Theologie," *JBT* 2 (1987): 33-57. Similar complications exist for New Testament theology, and perhaps also for systematic theology. For example, Folk Wagner has recently argued for greater clarity about the role of the history of theology in warranting systematic theology's claims ("Zur Theologiegeschichte des 19. und 20. Jahrhunderts," *TRu* 53 [1988]: 113-200).

3   It could be otherwise. Arguments about biblical theology could be made on methodological grounds: it must remain independent of theology in order to preserve its scientific or objective character as an independent historical-critical discipline, for example. The same argument could have a theological justification, of course. See Gerhard Ebeling, "The Meaning of 'Biblical Theology'," *Word and Faith* (Philadelphia: Fortress Press, 1963), 79-97; cf. also his seminal essay, "The Significance of the Critical Historical Method for Church and Theology in Portestantism," ibid., 19-61.

4   I have attempted to put this proposal into practice in "Isaiah's Creation Theology," *Ex Auditu* 3 (1987): 54-71. The present essay can be understood as a rationale for what I have done there.

5   I agree entirely with Jon Levenson that biblical theology—if it has the Bible as its context—is either Jewish or Christian; it cannot be neutral between them, if only because there is no neutrality on the question of what "Bible" includes, and to what it must be related ("The Eighth Principle of Judaism and the Literary Simultaneity of Scripture," *JR* 68 [1988]: 222-25). His essay is of cardinal importance for biblical theology. See also his "Why Jews are not Interested in Biblical Theology," in *Judaic Perspectives on Ancient Israel*, ed. J. Neusner, B. A. Levine, E. S. Frerichs (Philadelphia: Fortress Press, 1987), 281-307. There is no need to complicate matters further by trying here to define the distinction between systematic and dogmatic theology; the distinctions theologians draw between between them are sometimes as polemical in intent as that between biblical and systematic theology. Hans-Joachim Kraus offers one such polemical distinction, in favor of systematic over dogmatic theology (*Systematische Theologie* [Neukirchen-Vluyn: Neukirchener Verlag, 1983], 113-

15). His argument demonstrates how vastly the theological context in Europe changed over the half-century since Barth began writing his *Church Dogmatics*. In any event, I will not be careful, in this essay, to distinguish between systematic and dogmatic theology; but I will always have in mind something roughly equivalent to "specifically Christian theology," perhaps in a particularly Protestant mode.

6   For details, see Andrew L. Drummond, *German Protestantism Since Luther* (London: Epworth Press, 1951), 11-35.

7   Hans-Joachim Kraus, *Die Biblische Theologie* (Neukirchen-Vluyn: Nuekirchener Verlag, 1970), 20. Kraus is here describing the *Collegium Biblicum* of Sebastian Schmidt (1671). The fuller title of Schmidt's books is illuminating: "in quo dicta Veteris et Nova Testamenti iuxta sierem locorum communium theologicorum explicantur." The theological *loci* (topics) that Schmidt proposed to explicate, in relation to their Old and New Testament *dicta* (texts), were of a distinctly Protestant character.

8   Richard A. Muller, *Post-Reformation Dogmatics*, vol. 1: *Prolegomena to Theology* (Grand Rapids: Baker, 1987) offers a sympathetic and immensely rewarding account of the Protestant dogmaticians.

9   On the pietistic character of biblical theology see Kraus, *Die Biblische Theologie*, 20-26.

10   C. F. Ammon wrote a biblical theology in 1792, revised as *Biblische Theologie*, 3 vols. (Erlangen: J. J. Palin, 1801-1802). The unstable relationship between pietism and rationalism can be seen (1) in the priority accorded religion over theology, and (2) in the use of rationalistic criteria to determine what in the Bible is abidingly useful for religion.

11   The relevant portion of Gabler's address has been translated and published by John H. Sandys-Wunsch and Laurence Eldredge, "J. P. Gabler and the Distinction between Biblical and Dogmatic Theology," *SJT* 33 (1980): 133-58.

12   According to Gabler, biblical theology yields "truth" by following the historical investigation of the Bible with a philosophical operation, which distinguishes from among the Bible's statements those that agree with the universal truths of reason. Those biblical statements failing this test Gabler assigned to the realm of the merely historical. I have treated Gabler at greater length in "Biblical Theology: Situating the Discipline," *Understanding the Word* (JSOTSS 37; Sheffield: JSOT Press, 1985): 37-62.

13   This is especially true of Hermann Gunkel, the major figure in the school. See his programmatic essay, "Ziele und Methoden der Erkl_rung des Alten Testamentes," *Reden und Aufsätze* (G_ttingen: Vandenhoeck & Ruprecht, 1913), 11-29. Werner Klatt has offered a thorough account of Gunkel and his context, in *Hermann Gunkel: Zu seiner Theologie der Relgionsgeschichte und zur Entstehung der formgeschichtlichen Methode*, FRLANT 100 (Göttingen: Vandenhoeck & Ruprecht, 1969).

14   Brevard Childs chronicles this movement, in his *Biblical Theology in Crisis* (Philadelphia: Westminster, 1970).

15   An obvious but not unusual example is W. M. L. de Wette, who made significant contributions to both critical studies of the Bible and theology. His biblical theology (first published in 1813) and his dogmatics are bound together in one volume as a *Lehrbuch der christlichen Dogmatik* (Berlin: G. Reimer, 1831).

16   The first was Wolfgang Jacob Christmann's *Teutsche Biblische Theologie*, in 1629 (Kraus, *Biblische Theologie*, 20). Apparently, no copies of the book have survived.

17   *Reformed Dogmatics*, 63 (emphasis mine).

18   G. R. Evans, *The Language and Logic of the Bible: The Road to the Reformation* (Cambridge: Cambridge University Press, 1985); Frank Talmage, "Keep Your Sons from Scripture: The Bible in Medieval Jewish Scholarship and Spirituality," *Understanding Scripture: Explorations of Jewish and Christian Traditions of Interpretation*, ed. Clemens Thoma and Michael Wyschogrod (New York: Paulist Press, 1987), 88. Brian Gerrish understands the change in Calvin's *Institutes* betwee 1536 and 1539 to be a change in the direction of "explicitly *biblical* theology" ("Nature and the Theater of Redemption: Schleiermacher on Christian Dogmatics and the Creation Story," *Ex Auditu* 3 [1987]: 121, emphasis mine. Unfortunately, the published version drops a line, in the crucial passage, from the typescript of Gerrish's address). This judgment depends, of course, on what we mean by biblical (and by systematic) theology. I would see in the editions of Calvin's *Institutes* progress in the direction of a systematic theology that was increasingly biblical (see Elsie Anne McKee, "Exegesis, Theology, and Development in Calvin's *Institutio*: A Methodological Suggestion," in *Probing the Reformed Tradition: Historical Studies in Honor of Edward A. Dowey*, ed. E. A. McKee and B. G. Armstrong [Louisville: Westminster/John Knox Press, 1989], 154-73, and my essay, "We Believe in God . . . Maker of Heaven and Earth: Metaphor, Scripture, and Theology," forthcoming in *HBT*).

19   It need not be only a historical discipline. What matters, for this part of the discussion, is that biblical studies is pursued, quite legitimately, without principled regard for its relation to systematic theology. Robert Oden may be correct in claiming (a) that biblical studies should be pursued in independence from theology, and (b) that what he calls "the theological tradition" has continued to dominate biblical studies (*The Bible Without Theology* [San Francisco: Harper & Row, 1987]). However, I want to insist on a pair of distinctions. First, being a biblical scholar influenced by theology, or by whatever counts as "the theological tradition," is different from relating biblical studies to systematic theology. Second, one may proceed in self-conscious independence from systematic theology while still regarding one's work as important for theology, or for Christian faith, or for the church, etc. I would hazard the guess that a large percentage of those who today consider themselves biblical scholars would fall into at least the latter category, if only because they teach in seminaries or divinity schools.

would hazard the guess that a large percentage of those who today consider themselves biblical scholars would fall into at least the latter category, if only because they teach in seminaries or divinity schools.

20   This image is give perhaps its clearest expression by D. G. C. von Cölln, in his *Die biblische Theologie des Alten Testaments*, 2 vols (Leipzig: J. A. Barth, 1836), 1:4-12). It is customary to describe J. P. Gabler as holding this view, and even to name him as its principal sponsor (Gerhard Hasel, *Old Testament Theology: Basic Issues in the Current Debate*, third ed. [Grand Rapids: Eerdmans, 1982], 21-22, 78).   See above, note 12, for a contrasting interpretation of Gabler.

21   I have done so previously, in "What Krister Stendahl 'Meant'—A Normative Critique of 'Descriptive Biblical Theology'," *HBT* 8 (1986): 61-98. That article is a critique of Krister Stendahl's argument in "Methodology in the Study of Biblical Theology," *The Bible in Modern Scholarship* (ed. J. P. Hyatt; Nashville: Abingdon, 1965), 196-209.   However, what I have to say, in this paragraph, about the image of a "transaction" between biblical and systematic theology does not strictly apply to Stendahl; he has a view (or a proposal) about systematic theology that does not require it.

22   See the comments of Dietrich Ritschl, in "'Whare,' 'reine,' oder 'neue' Biblische Theologie," *JBT* 1 (1986): 135-50, especially p. 141.

23   This is not to say that systematic theologians never make use of historical investigation of the Bible.   Edward Farley, for example, points to historical criticism as one of the factors in the collapse of "the house of authority," on which his theological proposal depends (*Ecclesial Reflection: An Anatomy of Theological Method* [Philadelphia: Fortress Press, 1982], 136-52). But that would be, and is for Farley, just a reason *not* to ground systematic theology in historical investigation of the Bible.   In a totally different direction, Karl Barth makes repeated (and not always negative) reference to historical-critical biblical scholarship (e.g., *Church Dogmatics*, vol. 1:2 [Edinburgh: T. & T. Clark, 1956], 494).   It would be evident nonsense to claim that the volumes of Barth's *Dogmatics* are an elaboration of what historical investigation of the Bible had uncovered.

24   The "if" is to be taken seriously: I do not imply that this always is or that it must be the case.   Wilhelm Wrede was consistent in this regard; he considered the issue meaningless for biblical theology: "How the systematic theologian gets on with its results and deals with them—that his is own affair" ("The Task and Methods of 'New Testament Theology'," in *The Nature of New Testament Theology*, ed. Robert Morgan, SBT, 25 [London: SCM Press, 1973], 69. Wrede's address was first published in 1897).   See Friedrich Mildenberger's remarks on Wrede's conception of biblical theology, in *Theology of the Lutheran Confessions* (Philadelphia: Fortress Press, 1983), 215-16.

25   M. H. Goshen-Gottstein comments on an analogous relationship for Jewish study of Tanakh ("Tanakh Theology," pp. 627-30). He observes as well that the issues are different between Judaism and Christianity. This possibility worried William A. Irwin right at the beginning of the biblical theology

movement. In a letter responding to James D. Smart's approbation of Old Testament theology's renewal (Smart, "The Death and Rebirth of Old Testament Theology," *JR* 23 [1943]: 1-11, 125-36), Irwin asks whether we are to have "a Jewish and a Mohammedan and a Hindu" Old Testament theology, in addition to a Christian one. In that prospect, Irwin suggests that Old Testament theology be "relegated to the limbo of all subjective dogmatics" ("Old Testament Theology—Criticism of Dr. Smart's Article," ibid., 286).

26   This claim is made only for biblical theology since the eighteenth century. Since then, biblical theology has been joined with historical interpretation of the Bible (L. F. O. Baumgarten-Crusius, *Grundzüge der biblischen Theologie* [Jena: Frommann, 1828], 4). Prior to that time, history would not have been the focus of attention. However, the medieval debate regarding the appropriateness of classical methods in theology provided an analogous question (See G. R. Evans, *Old Arts and New Theology: The Beginnings of Theology as an Academic Discipline* [Oxford: Clarendon, 1980]).

27   Farley, *The Fragility of Knowledge*, 106. Farley's criticism is not limited to the movement of a generation ago; it is more general and more radical, but sometimes less profound, than that. For example, he says that "scholars working in the biblical fields act as if the old federal theology of covenants were still intact when they continue to speak about the Old Testament and the New Testament. This nomenclature disguises the historical-critical shift they take for granted" (ibid.).

28   Such a claim would be appropriate, in varying degrees, regarding nineteenth-century theologians, ranging from Gabler and de Wette to Vatke and Hofmann. It would be appropriate because these theologians incorporated philosophy—or, in the case of Hofmann, theology—within biblical theology itself, just in order to determine what in (or about) Scripture's content is true (see my essay, "From Timeless Ideas to the Essence of Religion," in *The Flowering of Old Testament Theology*, ed. B. C. Ollenburger, E. A. Martens, Gerhard Hasel [Winona Lake: Eisenbrauns, forthcoming]). On these grounds, they would be less susceptible to Farley's formal criticism than would be the biblical theologians he apparaently has in mind. Of course, Farley is himself a good deal more insistent on raising "the truth question" than he is clear on how to get it answered.

29   It would be just as pertinent if the methods were, for example, literary or structural or post-structural. See Burke O. Long, "A Figure at the Gate: Readers, Reading, and Biblical Theologians," in *Canon, Theology, and Old Testament Interpretation*, ed. G. M. Tucker, D. L. Petersen, R. R. Wilson (Philadelphia: Fortress Press, 1988), 166-86; Regina M. Schwartz, "Introduction: On Biblical Criticism," in *The Book and the Text: The Bible and Literary Theory*, ed. Regina M. Schwartz (Oxford: Basil Blackwell, 1990), 1-15.

30   From among Barr's extensive corpus, see especially *Semantics of Biblical Language* (London: Oxford University Press, 1961); *Old and New in Interpretation* (London: SCM Press, 1966, 1982); *The Bible in the Modern World* (London: SCM Press, 1973); *Does Biblical Study Still Belong to Theology?*

31   In *The Hermeneutical Quest: Essays in Honor of James Luther Mays*, ed. D. G. Miller (Allison Park, PA: Pickwick Press, 1986), 11-45.

32   To be sure, Barr has already conflated, somewhat prejudicially, the content of the Bible—the "actual biblical material"—and the activity of exegesis. The point of that conflation seems to be to insure that historical-critical exegesis will retain the mandate for determining what is the actual biblical material. In his earlier critique of Karl Barth, Barr proceeded in the same way. Of Barth's biblical interpretation, Barr said "the things said in the intepretation are just not there in the text, if one follows the linguistic form of the text" (*Old and New in Interpretation*, 94). And Barr insists that this has nothing to do with Barth's "lack of historical criticism" (ibid.). I do not know how the issue could be resolved by appeal to the text's "linguistic form," unless there were some means (Barr's or Barth's or some other) of determining what that form is. See also Levenson's comments, in "The Eighth Principle of Judaism," 213.

33   Eberhard Jüngel, *The Doctrine of the Trinity: God's Being is in Becoming* (Grand Rapids: Wm. B. Eerdmans, 1976).

34   Theology may proceed apart from any foundational appeal to Scripture, as is evident from some contemporary theologies. In Christian theology, however, even those theologies that make no foundational appeal to Scripture often say why this is the case, and thus make some policy statement with respect to Scripture. See as an example Sallie McFague, *Models of God: Theology for an Ecological, Nuclear Age* (Philadelphia: Fortress Press, 1987), 42-45.

35   By "practical interpretative work" I take Barr to mean something roughly equivalent to "actual biblical material" (13). That is, practical intepretative work is the kind of exegesis Barr and his colleagues do, and the actual biblical material is determined by just that exegetical work. Barr is not explicit about this, but he implies that the "practical interpretative work" critical exegesis does is uniquely fitted to the "actual biblical material."

36   It is important to observe the logical difference between (1) refusing to ground remarks about Jesus exclusively in the results of historical inquiry, and (2) refusing to make any use, or to take any account, of historical inquiry. The first refusal does not entail the second. S. W. Sykes makes a similar point in his "Introduction" to *Karl Barth: Centenary Essays*, ed. S. W. Sykes (Cambridge: Cambridge University Press, 1989), 11.

37   One part of its importance lies in the weight it grants to the actual practice of historical inquiry, which varies greatly from one era to the next, and even in the same era. Theologians cannot prescribe what historians should do, but they may find some kinds of historical inquiry more congenial to theology than others. Indeed, theologians may revise their theological method on the basis of one kind of historical inquiry, as Wolfhart Panneberg once did on the basis of Gerhard von Rad's history of traditions (*Offenbarung als Geschichte*, ed. Wolfhart Pannenberg, third ed. [Göttingen: Vandenhoeck & Ruprecht, 3rd edition, 1965], 132-48).

[38]   The Theological Case Against Biblical Theology," in *Canon, Theology and Old Testament Interpretation: Essays in Honor of Brevard S. Childs*, ed. G. M. Tucker, D. L. Petersen, R. R. Wilson (Philadelphia: Fortress Press, 1988), 5.

[39]   G. Ernest Wright, "History and Reality: The Importance of Israel's 'Historical Symbols' for the Christian Faith," in *The Old Testament and Christian Faith*, ed. B. W. Anderson (New York: Herder & Herder, 1969), 176-99; "Historical Knowledge and Revelation," in *Translating and Understanding the Old Testament*, ed. H. T. Frank, W. L. Reed (Nashville: Abingdon Press, 1970), 279-303. Rowley himself says that "The Old Testament theologian must remember all the work done by the historian, and the study of the history of Old Testament religion must continue side by side with the study of the theology of the Old Testament" (*The Faith of Israel* [London: SCM Press, 1956], 15). See also Childs, *Biblical Theology in Crisis*, 41-42.

[40]   Elsewhere, Barr says that "biblical theology never advanced or demanded criteria or procedures which differ from the treatment of evidence in a descriptive treatment of the same phenomena," and he is referring in this context to "historical description" ("Trends and Prospects in Biblical Theology," *JTS* 25 [1974]: 278). This seems at odds with his claims in the essay under discussion.

[41]   See Childs, *Biblical Theology in Crisis*, 51-52. G. Ernest Wright was vehement in his criticism of what he took to be Barthian "Christomonism." See his *The Old Testament and Theology* (New York: Harper & Row, 1969). Barr's Oxford colleague, John Barton, follows Barr (without referring to him) in suggsting that those who want to reconsider the relation of biblical studies to theology are motivated by "a prior commitment to a Barthian approach to theology" ("Should Old Testament Study be More Theological?" *ET* 100 [1989]: 445).

[42]   *Biblical Theology in Crisis*, 21. The term "Free Church" is somewhat elusive. Childs is not speaking here of, say, Mennonites or Baptists.

[43]   *TToday* 1 (1944-45): 47-58. The quote is from p. 55 (emphasis his).

[44]   Childs, *Biblical Theology in Crisis*, 21 (emphasis mine).

[45]   Barr says that "the authority of the Bible . . . must be *shown* on sufficient grounds" ("Trends in Biblical Theology," 282). Charles M. Wood seems to suggest something similar. He locates biblical theology within historical theology, because in his view, theology does not assume that "the church has acted rightly" in assigning the Bible a function in judging "the representativeness of Christian witness." It is "always open to question," he says, whether the church has acted rightly in this assignment (*Vision and Discernment* [Atlanta: Scholars Press, 1985], 43).

[46]   The most imposing use of sociological theory by a biblical scholar is Norman Gottwald's. On its basis he even advocates a revised definition of theology: theology is "a scientific study of the divine manifestation in history" (*The Tribes of Yahweh* [Maryknoll: Orbis Books, 1979], 794, note 100).

[47]   *Biblical Theology in Crisis*, 95.

48   Karl Barth, *Church Dogmatics*, vol. 1:1 (Edinburgh: T. & T. Clark, 1975), 16.

49   Ibid., 11.

50   David Kelsey discuess similar issues clearly and at length in his *The Uses of Scripture in Recent Theology*: (Philadelphia: Fortress Press, 1972). Barr refers (19) in this connection to Dietrich Ritschl's observation that very little of the Bible, including the Pauline letters, is really "theology" (Ritschl, *The Logic of Theology* [London: SCM Press, 1986], 68-69). That observation is not new and is strictly beside the point. (Ritschl says that his observation on this point has "been guided by" his "conversation partner and friend James Barr" [Ritschl, 69].) That theology should have the Bible as its criterion does not depend, if it has ever depended, on the Bible constituting "a material, tangible and directly applicable collection of doctrinal statements" (ibid., 68). Even the post-Reformation scholastics recognized that. Biblical theology, we may say, *depends* on this recognition, a self-evident one, in support of which Barr invokes Ritschl (who invokes Barr) to undermine biblical theology. I have no objection to Ritschl's commendation of patristics as a neglected focus of Christian theology, though I have no idea why he thinks this would avoid "fideistic and fundamentalistic absolutism and a biblicistic postivism of revelation" (ibid., 74-75), despite the daunting mass of opprobrium.

51   *Mutatis mutandis*, the same is true of Judaism, at least on Goshen-Gottstein's account ("Tanakh Theology").

52   For purposes of this argument we do not need to prove, in other words, that this serves as a generalization for all Christian communities, and we do not need to argue—in this context—that it *should* so serve. See note 44, above.

53   On this definition, Christian communities may be committed to one or another version of foundationalism. Whether they are so in fact will depend on the specific accounts Christian communities, or their theologians, offer of (or for) their dependence on the Bible as Scripture. (For example, see Ronald F. Thiemann, *Revelation and Theology: The Gospel as Narrated Promise* [Notre Dame: University of Notre Dame Press, 1985]; John Sykes, "Narrative Accounts of Biblical Authority: The Need for a Doctrine of Revelation," MT 5 [1989]: 327-42; L. Gregory Jones, "A Response to Sykes: Revelation and the Practices of Interpreting Scripture," MT 5 [1989]: 343-48. On philosophical foundationalism see Alvin Plantinga, "Coherentism and the Evidentialist Objection to Belief in God," *Rationality, Religious Belief, and Moral Commitment*, ed. R. Audi, W. J. Wainwright (Ithaca: Cornell U. Press, 1986), 109-38; William P. Alston, "Plantinga's Epistemology of Religous Belief," *Alvin Plantinga*, ed. J. E. Tomberlin, P. Van Inwagen (Dordrecht: D. Reidel, 1985], 289-309.) It is sufficient here to observe that the foundational importance of texts does not entail foundationalism, and it may even be an antidote.

54   Biblical Narrative and Theological Anthropology," in *Scriptural Authority and Narrative Interpretation*, ed. Garrett Green (Philadelphia: Fortress Press, 1987), 137. I made a similar point in "Biblical Theology: Situating the Discipline," 53.

55   More recently, it is also Gerhard Hasel's view ("The Relationship Between Biblical theology and Systematic Theology," *TJ* 5 [1984]: 127). Hasel says that "biblical theology is foundational for systematic theology, if systematic theology is to receive its normative authority from Scripture." While Hasel insists that biblical theology should not derive its "structure" from "the loci of systematic theology" (ibid., 126), and that systematic theology "is not made superfluous through biblical theology" (ibid., 127), he does not say from where systematic theology should derive its *loci*, or why it should have them—or why systematic theology is not strictly superfluous.

56   Hans W. Frei, in "Barth and Schleiermacher: Divergence and Convergence," *Barth and Schleiermacher: Beyond the Impasse?* ed. J. O. Duke and R. F. Streetman (Philadelphia: Fortress Press, 1988), 79.

57   *The Christian Faith* (Edinburgh: T. & T. Clark, 1928), #27, p. 116. See B. A. Gerrish, "Nature and the Theater of Redemption," 122-23. I will continue to speak of systematic theology, even though the term is not strictly accurate in reference to Schleiermacher. If we were to pursue the argument further, we would need to make more careful distinctions, and to face the possible liabilities in conceiving systematic theology as *Glaubenslehre*. Here I have in mind Anders Jeffner's criticisms of the "flight to descriptivism" in dogmatics: "Instead of asserting a given theological doctrine, the theologian can simply describe it, adding that this is the doctrine of the Christian Church or of a specific Christian Church. To establish the truth of such a description, you need none of the special theological criteria of truth" (*Theology and Integration* [Uppsala: Almqvist & Wiksell, 1987], 37-38, quoted in Vincent Brümmer, "Philosophical Theology as Conceptual Recollection," *NZST* 32 [1990], 68). Scripture will be included in whatever are those "theological critiera of truth," and on that basis I continue to find Schleiermacher useful in arguing about biblical theology's relation to systematic theology.

58   *Christian Faith*, #27, p. 113. On p. 115, Schleiermacher says why, in his view, the Old Testament cannot independently attest any genuinely Christian doctrine, and is thus "simply a superfluous authority for dogmatics." I see no reason to follow him on this point, and many reasons not to do so.

59   See Manfred Oeming, *Gesamtbiblische Theologien der Gegenwart*, second ed. (Suttgart: W. Kohlhammer, 1987), 225.

60   Gerrish notes that while Schleiermacher's method is "pscyhologizing,' "it is a collective consciousness that occupies his attention" and not an individual consciousness or self-consciousness ("Nature and the Theater of Redemption," 122). On Ronald Thiemann's definition of "nonfoundational theology"—it is "located squarely within Christian tradition and seeks to 're-describe' the internal logic of the Christian faith" (*Revelation and Theology*, 75)—Schleiermacher's *Glaubenslehre* is nonfoundational, as Gerrish argues against Thiemann (Gerrish, 128-32). Whether Schleiermacher himself was, in other respects, a foundationalist is quite another question. There is nothing self-contradictory, I suppose, in conceiving and practicing dogmatic theology nonfoundationally, while being at the same time a philosophical foundation-

self-contradictory, I suppose, in conceiving and practicing dogmatic theology nonfoundationally, while being at the same time a philosophical foundationalist. Still, some of his successors did think of this as an inconsistency within Schleiermacher's work.

61   Quoting Kelsey, "Theological Anthropology," 137. One may propose that a Christian community's first-order discourse is taken up as, or incorporated within, systematic theology's second-order discourse. In this case, systematic theology's discourse—even if its vocabulary parallels that of a Christian community's—would be "a-semantic" (Kathryn Tanner, "Theology and the Plain Sense," *Scriptural Authority and Narrative Interpretation* (ed. Garrett Green: Philadelphia: Fortress, 1987) 62.

62   David Kelsey (*The Uses of Scripture*, 192-97) and William Placher (*Unapologetic Theology* [Louisville: Westminster/John Knox Press, 1989], 123-37) stress the importance of patterns in Scripture, or the patterns of biblical narrative, for theology. Sometimes Christian communities make an explicit judgment about Scripture's wholeness, as in a catechism. In other cases, such judgments are both *ad hoc* and implicit.

63   Rebecca Chopp speaks of the "constant deliberation of life together in Word and with the Scriptures" as "the rhetorical nature of community, the ongoing deliberation of who it is, what it does, where it is going, the nature of its past" (*The Power to Speak: Feminism, Language, God* [New York: Crossroad, 1989], 91).

64   No Christian community can be understood exhaustively, or reductively, as a commentary on, or an interpretation of, Scripture. Any such community could also be understood as a commentary on, or even as an inscription of, the prevailing culture, for example.

65   In fact, it is formally similar to Gabler's proposal, which gave birth to biblical theology in 1787—only formally similar, since it assumes a conception of theology markedly different from Gabler's own. See also Robert Morgan, in Morgan and John Barton, *Biblical Interpretation* (Oxford: Oxford U. Press, 1988); Klaus Berger, *Heremeneutik des Neuen Testaments* (Gütersloh: Gerd Mohn, 1988).

66   This does not assume a narrow understanding of 'community.' A given community may be as broad as the whole Christian church. No matter how narrowly theology may work in a given instance—Schleiermacher's for example—one could argue that its *horizon* should never be narrower than the church catholic. Its horizon should never be so narrow as one public culture, or as a single subculture within it, say an academic one.

67   *Ethics After Babel: The Languages of Morals and Their Discontents* (Boston: Beacon, 1988), 28.

68   *The Christian Faith*, #109, p. 502.

69   He speaks, in this regard, of "all doctrines which are dogmatic expressions of that which, in the public proceedings of the Church (even if only in certain regions of it), can be put forward as a presentation of its common piety without provoking dissension and schism" (*The Christian Faith*, #19, pp. 89-90).

⁷⁰ I have been assuming distinctions among kerygmatic, rhetorical, and discursive practices, and identifying theology with the latter. However, it should be clear that their boundaries are fluid and porous, and that they are mutually dependent.

⁷¹ A similar theme is struck, with somewhat different accents, by Oeming, *Gesamtbiblische Theologien*, 223-37; Friedrich Mildenberger, "Systematisch-theologische Randbemerkungen zur Diskussion um eine Biblische Theologie," in *Zugang zur Theologie: Fundamentaltheologische Beiträge*, ed. F. Mildenberger, J. Track (Göttingen: Vandenhoeck & Ruprecht, 1979), 11-32; "Biblische Theologie als kirchliche Schriftauslegung," *JBT* 1 (1986): 151-62; Ulrich Kühn, "Die Kirche als Ort der Theologie," *KD* 31 (1985): 98-115. The concerns of these theologians represent a sometimes striking difference from what Richard H. Roberts describes as "North American university theology," which "has moved decisively in the direction of an academicist liberalism," and away from a "healthy insistence upon the Church and witness-related character of Christian theology." Roberts says that "the consequences of this distancing of the pursuit of theology as a liberal arts discipline from a responsible relationship with tradition and equally from the active life of the Church may well be considerable" ("The Reception of the Theology of Karl Barth in the Anglo-Saxon World: History, Typology, and Prospect," in *Karl Barth: Centenary Essays*, 154-55).

⁷² *The Christian Faith*, # 19, p. 90. Any dogmatic system, he says, "of purely and entirely individual opinions and views, which, even if really Christian, did not link themselves at all to the expressions used in the Church for the communication of religion, would always be regarded as simply a private confession and not as a dogmatic presentation, until there came to be attached to it a like-minded society, and there thus arose a public preaching and communication of religion which found its norm in that doctrine" (ibid.).

⁷³ I set out what I understand by 'descriptive' and 'normative' in "What Krister Stendahl 'Meant'" (see above, note 21).

⁷⁴ Janet Martin Soskice, *Metaphor and Religious Language* (Oxford: Oxford University Press, 1985), 127, 149. See also Kripke, "Naming and Necessity," in *Semantics of Natural Language*, ed. D. Davidson and G. Harman (Dordrecht: D. Reidel, 1972), 253-355; *Wittgenstein on Rules and Private Language* (Cambridge: Harvard U. Press, 1982). I do not believe Soskice's use of Kripke is undermined by Colin McGinn's criticisms of him in *Wittgenstein on Meaning* (New York: Blackwells, 1984), 184-200.

⁷⁵ Soskice, *Metaphor and Religious Language*, p. 149.

⁷⁶ Ibid., 150. In "Biblical Theology: Situating the Discipline," I made a similar point: "Any disciplined form of inquiry...presupposes a community of interest whose methods and procedures rest upon commonly held assumptions that have endured over time (a tradition); and the phenomena to which inquiry is directed are chosen, or perhaps shaped, on the basis of their relevance to that community" (p. 52).

77 Jesper Høgenhaven, *Problems and Prospects of Old Testament Theology* (Sheffield: JSOT Press, 1988), 126, note 1.

78 Much of what William A. Christian, Sr., says about philosophers of religion applies in the present context: "In the past two centuries there has been a tendency for philosophers of religion to take the religious reflections of individuals as their subject matter. One reason is that in this period the ties of individuals to religious communities have often been loosed or broken. So individuals who continue to have active religious interests have tended to look elsewhere than to their own communities for inspiration and guidance. In response, many philosophers of religion have undertaken to offer inspiration and guidance to such individuals in their religious reflections. So a good deal of what has been produced under the auspices of philosophy of religion has been religious philosophy" (*Doctrines of Religious Communities: A Philosophical Study* [New Haven: Yale University Press, 1987], 229).

79 References to taking the texts "on their own terms" obscure this. Cf. Sallie McFague, *Models of God* (Philadelphia: Fortress, 1987), 43; John Barton, *People of the Book* (Louisville: Westminster/ John Knox, 1988), 17. Any interpretation, any description, of a text is in—and on—terms other than its own. Especially instructive in this regard are the remarks by Tanner on Scripture's 'plain sense' (see below).

80 "Should Old Testament Theology be More Theological?" 448.

81 "Exegesis as a Theological Discipline," 35.

82 See Ollenburger, "Biblical Theology: Situating the Discipline," 44-46.

83 Jeffrey Stout, "The Relativity of Interpretation," *The Monist* 69 (1986): 103-18 (see especially pp. 112-16). Stout deals with interpretation generally, and not at all with biblical interpretation (his first example in these pages is Herbert Fingarette's interpretation of Confuscius). The remainder of this paragraph depends heavily on Stout's article.

84 Ibid., 113.

85 "Theology and the Plain Sense," p. 72.

86 For a contrasting approach, see Heikki Räisänen, *Beyond New Testament Theology: A Story and a Programme* (London: SCM Press, 1990).

87 In Gilson's original, "Philosophy always buries its undertakers" (quoted by Hilary Putnam, in *Philosophical Papers*, vol 3: *Realism and Reason* [Cambridge: Cambridge University Press, 1983], 303).